Simple Times, Simple Pleasures

Growing up in the 1930s and '40s:
A Scrapbook of Memories

By

Helen Elizabeth (Treece) Merrell

This is an account of my childhood from my memories, some of my Aunt Leola Gilmore's memories and those of my brothers and sisters that were written for our family reunion in 1987.

Other books by Ray and Helen Merrell: *My Three Years in the Marine Corps,* WWII, 1996; and *My Three Years in the Marine Corps,* WWII, revised second edition, 2004.

For more information, please contact the author at:
helen42146@hotmail.com

ISBN 1-58597-281-9

Library of Congress Control Number: 2004095300

A division of Squire Publishers, Inc.
4500 College Blvd.
Leawood, KS 66211
1/888/888/7696
www.leatherspublishing.com

Dedicated to
our daughter, Deborah Sue Hopper,
and
our son, Robert Alan Merrell;

and in loving memory of my mother, father,
sisters, brothers and my one living sister,
Leola Marie (Mildred) Wheeler.

ACKNOWLEDGMENTS

Special thoughts, love and thanks to my sister-in-law, Elsie (Thomas) Treece, and my aunt, Leola Gilmore, who contributed pictures and stories. Most of all, to my husband for his patience while I took the time to write this book, and for the love he has always shown me.

.

CONTENTS

I

Childhood and Growing Up

AT FIVE O'CLOCK in the morning all my brothers and sisters were standing on the stairway anxiously waiting. It was January 25th, 1927, at our beautiful Elm Ridge farm home, high on a hill near Sweet Springs, Missouri. Our beloved family doctor, Dr. Harrison, had been called and was in an upstairs bedroom. Just a little while later my father came down the stairs with a smile on his face and a twinkle in his eye. He was bringing news of a new baby sister, born at 5:10 a.m. and named Helen Elizabeth in honor of two of my brothers' and sisters' favorite teachers at Armentrout School.

My father was one of the directors at Armentrout School where

Elm Ridge, 1919.

1

Elm Ridge porch. L-R: Mother, Grandpa Treece, with baby Leola Marie, Rose, Mary, Sue.

they attended, and he signed the teachers' paychecks. I was lucky to have (in age order) three older brothers, John, Joe and Francis, and three older sisters, Mary, Rose and Mildred. Mildred's name was actually Leola Marie, but my Grandfather Treece didn't like the name so he called her Mildred, and the rest of us did also.

At the time I was born, my dad had a Model T Ford with isinglass windows. There had been a tornado at the farm earlier that in its fury had blown the shed where the car was parked down the hill, but left the car untouched and standing proud.

My mom and dad had sold their farm northeast of Sweet Springs and moved to Elm Ridge Farm six years before. A lot of interesting things happened at Elm Ridge, and my brothers and sisters all had fond memories of their time there, along with some mishaps and capers. Like the time a

Picture taken at Grandma and Grandpa Gregg's in Independence, MO. Mildred, Rose, Mary, Joe (behind Mary), John, Francis. In front, George Gregg (a cousin), Helen.

Dad's Model T Ford. Aunt Georgia, Aunt Leola, Dad, Grandpa Gregg.

neighbor called to tell Mom that Francis and Mary were on top of a very tall barn. I can only imagine that frightening experience as they talked them down.

When I was three months old, we all had the measles at the same time. Mom had to carry me trying to get the measles to break out while taking care of all the other children. John was the first to heal; he then helped with the younger children. While we were ill our good neighbor, Raymond King, brought a big pot of soup and some pudding to us. My brothers and sisters always remembered how good it tasted.

Some time later Mildred was exposed to and had the chicken pox. She ended up with a scar right in the middle of her forehead. I never had the chicken pox, and I don't think any of the others did.

Our good Dr. Harrison would always come when called and stayed to visit and eat. He was a great doctor and a good friend. Francis had some kind of arthritis when he was quite young and had so much pain he had to be turned with a sheet. Dr. Harrison cured him, and years later Mom wondered what medicine he had used.

When I was two years old Mary's arm was broken while swinging with Alma Renken at Armentrout School. They were standing up trying to see how high they could go when the swing broke and

Alma fell on top of Mary. Mary was unconscious for about an hour. Dad was called and he took her to the doctor in Sweet Springs, then to the Marshall, Missouri hospital. Her arm was splintered and hard to set. They tried setting it many times, then decided it just couldn't be exact. She was right-handed and luckily it was her left arm that was broken. It did heal and was fine. Dad had a phone put in Armentrout School after that incident.

Joe and "Old Sue."

We had a shepherd dog named "Old Sue" who was a faithful companion to all. I don't remember Old Sue, but have heard a lot of stories about how she would be found sleeping beside John or Joe by the grape arbor, or standing guard down by the creek with them.

I don't know how old Mary was when John pulled her off a spreading viper snake. Mary always said, "John saved my life;" and I'm quite sure that is true.

Joe got his head caught in the rounds of the stair railing just as we were ready to go someplace. Dad immediately took his saw and sawed off one of the rounds so he could get his head out. The

Mary and "Old Sue."

rounds were so close together no one knew how he could get his head between them; they also said only Joe could have done that.

Dad built a large poultry house, and Mom had beautiful white geese. Occasionally we would have one for dinner. Mom also raised small chickens. There was a garage and machine shed, a blackberry patch north of the house, a grape arbor east of the garage, and a potato patch west of the big barn. Dad put stanchions in the west side of the barn for the milk cows. There was a concrete floor for the stalls.

The house at Elm Ridge had four large bedrooms upstairs, one parlor bedroom downstairs, a large living room, large dining room, large kitchen with a water pump and a full basement (or cellar) with inside entrance from the kitchen, and outside entrance from the porch.

My earliest memory is riding my tricycle around the big porch that was three-fourths of the way around the house. I was only three years old when we moved from Elm Ridge Farm back to the farm northeast of Sweet Springs. Then I rode my tricycle on the sidewalk from the house to the separator house. Mom said I kept wanting to go home so I could ride my tricycle around the wrap-around porch.

The people Dad had sold the farm to couldn't pay the mortgage, so Dad had to take it back and pay for it again. Before my family moved to Elm Ridge, they had called the farm "Blue Bell Farm."

The farm hadn't been taken care of; the fields had been washed

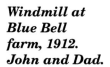

Windmill at Blue Bell farm, 1912. John and Dad.

Sidewalk from house to separator house. Garage on other side of fence.

away and there were enormous ditches to be filled. John remembered driving there in a wagon to cut trees, trim hedge fences, and getting poison ivy. Fences had to be rebuilt.

My dad and brothers worked very hard to get the farm back in good shape. They had lived at Elm Ridge for nine years.

Our farm home had a lot less room than the Elm Ridge Farm. Mom had to fit the furniture and everything in just so. There were three bedrooms, a living room, dining room and kitchen. The three boys slept in one room, the four girls in another. In the girls' room there was only room for a bed and a cot. Mary and I slept in the bed and Rose and Mildred on the cot. There was a clothes closet in one end of the room. In winter we had so many blankets and quilts on our bed to keep warm we could hardly turn over.

There was a big wood-burning pot-bellied stove in the living room and a wood-burning cook stove in the kitchen. The kitchen had a free-standing cabinet with a flour bin and a sugar bin. There was a small

Living room stove.

Something like our kitchen stove, with warming storage above. Wood box was beside stove.

table with a bucket and a dipper for our drinking water, and a wash pan.

There was a cistern (a tank underground for holding rainwater) with a pump outside the kitchen door, a smokehouse for Dad's sugar-cured hams, shoulders and bacon, and a cellar close by. The cellar had a potato bin and shelves for Mom's many jars of home canning. Eggs when gathered were taken to the cellar and put in egg cases. The cellar was also used to keep other things cool.

My favorite pastime at our new home (new to me) was making mud pies, using bird eggs for ingredients and red brick that I had pounded with a hammer into small grains for icing. I would then set the pies in the sun to bake.

I loved walking barefoot in the soft mud after a spring rain and feeling the mud ooze between my toes.

My childhood was during the Great Depression, droughts, dust

Blue Bell farm home where John, Joe, Francis and Mary were born.

7

Door to cellar in front, smokehouse behind.

storms and grasshopper plagues. When the depression hit, 35 percent of all Americans were out of work. Banks, insurance companies and businesses failed and locked their doors. During the depression we were happy with what we had; mostly we didn't even know what we didn't have. Anyway, we didn't worry about it.

The droughts of 1934 and 1936 turned several states into dust bowls. Big clouds of dust would roll through and it would get very dark. I remember Mom hanging wet towels over the windows and stuffing them in the window sills. That might have slowed the dust down some, but it still came in and would settle on everything.

Canned goods.

The grasshoppers were like a storm coming in they were so thick. They ate the corn and other crops, even ate the fence posts, chewed on the handles of pitchforks, shovels and all kinds of wood-handled tools. They certainly left their mark.

We would sleep outside on cots in the very hot weather we

8

seemed to have every summer. We had fun making a wish on the first star out at night, seeing shooting stars and watching the moon come up. We loved listening to the croaking of bullfrogs, noises of the crickets, hoot owls and other evening country sounds, and then waking up to the roosters crowing, cows mooing and birds chirping. Other sounds we loved hearing were the windmill turning, clucking of hens, peeping of baby chicks, cooing of pigeons and squealing of pigs.

Helen at side of separator house.

I always managed to have poison ivy every summer. I tried to get some relief by staying in the shade or sitting on a blanket under a shade tree. That didn't help much, but it was nice sitting there visiting and drinking ice tea or lemonade.

My big job was gathering the eggs. The trick was to try to keep the hens from pecking me. When I was a little younger, I was playing in the chickens' waterer and a rooster pecked me on the cheek. I still have the scar. The old rooster didn't live long after that as we had him for dinner that very same day.

My only other injury was hitting the back of my head on the corner of a block of wood while turning somersaults on a chinning bar. That caused a bad cut that soot and salt was applied to stop the bleeding.

Helen with doll.

I also carried wood from the wood pile to fill the wood box by the kitchen stove, and carried buckets of water from the deep well to drink and to water the chickens. Everyone had chores to do; there was no such thing as an allowance at that

9

Back row: John, Joe, Francis (behind Mary). Middle row: Dad, Rose, Mom, Mary. Front row: Helen, Mildred.

time, we just did what needed to be done.

We brushed our teeth with baking soda and salt. We had an outhouse with an old Sears Catalog. We washed our hands and faces in a wash pan and we bathed in a galvanized washtub in water heated on the wood cook stove. We played lots of tricks on each other, cut our feet and stubbed our toes, but had a great time growing up.

I was having such a good time one sunny morning swinging around a post on our front porch when my dad told me to stop. Well! I didn't see any reason to stop all that fun. My dad promptly

Our front porch.

Herndon Store.

spanked me, and that was quite a surprise. It was such a surprise that I even wet my pants and threw a fit of crying. I remember getting dry pants and hanging my wet ones on the clothesline. I can still see them hanging there, blowing in the breeze. It didn't take me long to get over that as Dad was going to the Herndon Store and I wanted to go with him. I knew he would buy me a sack of candy, and that's what he did. I had learned my lesson. That is the only spanking I remember getting. I knew my limits from then on — mostly, and I was thankful for his discipline — later.

Mom was always working. She had a big one-half acre garden on the other side of the barn, and one-half acre truck garden down by the creek. She took care of chickens and baby chickens in the spring. She canned hundreds of jars of fruit, vegetables, sauerkraut (made in a stone jar and then canned), pickles, pickle relish, preserves, jellies and meat. Her canned tenderloin and gravy were heaven to eat. She also made our clothes and lots of quilts on her old pedal Singer sewing machine.

Crooked Creek ran through our farm. There was a lane we walked down to get there. There was a lot of fishing in the creek. Mom and Dad had a truck garden close to the creek where they planted potatoes, sweet corn, watermelon, pumpkin and cantaloupe.

There was a huge ditch close to the creek. Old furniture, farm equipment and odds and ends were thrown into it. Some would probably be prized antiques today.

Mom and her chickens at young chickens' house.

Mom would pick blackberries, raspberries and gooseberries in the woods close to the creek, and I liked to pick wild flowers that bloomed there, like butter-cups, violets, boy's britches, lily of the valley, etc.

Mom would also pick lambs quarter, carpenter's square, wild lettuce, dock and mustard greens wherever it grew, usually carrying it in her apron back to the house.

The lane starts at the windmill (over the deep well) behind the barn and goes all the way to the creek. It was always fun walking, running, skipping, thinking, singing, planning or just plain daydreaming. I feel so fortunate to have been on the farm during my childhood. I surely have a charmed life; I have so many beautiful memories.

Mom cooked three big meals every day: breakfast, dinner and supper. We would wake up to the aroma of country sugar-cured ham and bacon frying in the big iron skillet. Mom always wore an apron and it served many purposes, like bringing in sweet corn

Mildred, Helen and McArthur. Chicken house in background.

Helen, Mildred, Rose, Mary, Francis, Joe, John, Mom, Dad, 1936.

for roasting ears, vegetables from the garden, eggs that might be found in unusual places and for shooing chickens. Later, when she had grandchildren, she carried Cheerios in her apron pockets for them. She would bake seven loaves of bread at a time. It was so good, especially the heel, when hot and fresh from the oven, spread with homemade butter and jelly or preserves. Mom always made damson, cherry, apricot and peach preserves, also watermelon preserves — that was one I could do without.

We had a big rectangular dark oak dining room table covered with a checked table cloth (white on Sunday), and each of us had our own place. Dad sat at one end and I sat beside him. Mom sat at the other end, the other three girls on one side and the three boys on the other. Dad always said the blessing. No chewing gum was allowed, but there was a lot of chewing gum stuck under the table, more in some places than others.

Mom would cut the chickens' heads off with a little hatchet, or wring their necks, dipped it in hot water until thoroughly wet, picked the feathers and pin feathers off, then cut it up on a little table under the walnut tree by the smokehouse. They were then put to soak in a stone crock in cold water and salt until time to fry. We had fried chicken a lot and always fresh vegetables from the garden and fruit from the orchard, always good fresh milk to drink,

Sisters: Helen, Mary, Rose, Mildred, 1936.

ice tea and lemonade, and the best of all, good fresh water from the deep well. Mom would ring the dinner bell that was on a post beside the smokehouse for Dad and whoever was working in the field to come in to eat. Aunt Leola said, "Nell (my mom) tried to teach me to wring a chicken's neck; I tried and the neck got longer and longer. I threw the chicken in the air, then had to run it down, and Nell grabbed her hatchet and away the neck went." Aunt Leola said she loved the farm but after spending summers on the farm made up her mind early in life not to marry a farmer.

During wheat harvest cooking for the men started early in the morning, baking six or seven pies of different kinds. I loved all of Mom's pies — two of my favorites were rhubarb/mulberry and gooseberry — then a big delicious meal. Mom had a small pie pan and she would bake an individual pie just for me. Of course, she did the same for my

Dinner bell beside smokehouse. Helen, Ray, Butch, 1946.

older brothers and sisters when they were the youngest. Come to think of it though, I was the youngest the longest. Wasn't I lucky! Someone (usually Mildred — she was the one I remember anyway) would take a lunch to the threshing crew mid-morning and mid-afternoon, as they started early and would run until almost dark. Cooking on the wood stove made it even more hot. Flies were plentiful, and with so many going in and out the doors, we would have to shoo them out the door with tea towels.

Sometimes when Mom made pies she would take the trimmings from the crust, sprinkle it with sugar and cinnamon, roll it and bake it. They were called toadies and were they good! Sure didn't last long.

I would help set the table, Mildred carried the dishes from the table to the kitchen, Mary and Rose washed and dried the dishes. Mary hated washing the dishes and would promise Rose most anything if she would wash them. She even hid in an apple tree one time to keep from washing the dishes.

Mom made a lot of school dresses, pajamas, aprons, tablecloths, curtains and quilts on her sewing machine. Many mills bagged livestock feed in material that could be reused as material, and a lot of my school dresses, and many other things, were made from that.

Mom and Dad made lye soap, a mixture of hog lard and lye, in a big 30-gallon cast-iron kettle. It was cooked for hours and stirred with a wooden paddle over a fire built in the chicken yard close to the separator house. When finished it was cooled, then cut into large bars to be used for scrubbing laundry on a large washboard. Washing was a big job, of course, having to heat water on the wood cook stove in a big copper kettle. Tubs were set up in the shade of a tree and most of the day was spent washing, stopping occasionally to do other chores. Clothes were rinsed well and hung on clothes lines, also on bushes and the fence in the sun if not enough room on the line. Bluing was used and the whites came out as white as snow. Sometimes in the colder weather the clothes would freeze dry on the lines and would be brought in as stiff as boards. When the weather was too wet or too cold the clothes had to be hung inside the house. Usually on those days Mom would have a

Copper kettle on wood cook stove.

big pot of vegetable soup simmering on the stove. That was a welcome aroma, especially when getting home from school.

Ironing was a big job; even socks, underwear, towels and sheets were ironed. Material was much different then and many shirts and dresses were starched with homemade starch. When they were dry, they were then sprinkled with water and rolled in a towel to dampen all over, then ironed. Flat irons were heated on the kitchen stove. One was used until it was no longer hot, then it was put back on the stove to reheat and another was used.

Dad worked from dawn till dusk putting in crops and taking care of them. There were cattle, horses and pigs to care for, fences to be kept mended, weeds to be cut, and the farm to be kept in good shape. Dad found a lot of Indian arrowheads, tomahawks and clay pipes while working the fields; he had a good collection but they were mostly lost by different ones taking them to school to show.

Milking had to be done morning and night. The boys helped when they were home; Mildred and Mary also helped in the field and to separate the milk and feed the animals.

Flat iron was heated on kitchen stove.

There was always work to do. Threshing wheat, baling hay and putting hay in the barn loft, cutting corn by the stalk and putting it in shocks for winter feed for the cattle, or shucking corn by hand. Joe said, "I always stood next to the wagon when John and Dad and I were gathering corn by hand and, guess what John and Dad always hit."

The milk was brought to the separator house and put in the big separator. There were two spouts; milk came out of the larger spout and cream out the smaller. The separated milk was used to mix with feed for the hogs, the cream was put in large cream cans and sold to the

5-gallon cream can.

creamery in Sweet Springs. Part of the milk that was not separated was used to drink, and on the rest cream would rise to the top of the milk. The milk was used to make cottage cheese, and the cream was used on hot oatmeal, peaches, strawberries or other fruit. It also was used for whipped cream, especially on Mom's strawberry shortcake, pumpkin pie, etc. Cream was used to put in the big stone churn with paddles to make butter, or to make homemade ice cream. Mom would make the ice cream mixture (my favorite was when she mashed bananas in with the mixture and made banana ice cream) put it in the ice cream can with the paddles, then put in the wooden freezer with salt and ice packed around the can. Then someone had to turn the handle until the cream was frozen. Many neighbors and friends would come by in the evening to enjoy eating ice cream with us.

I liked to go with Dad when he took cream to the creamery and cases of eggs to the produce house, owned by Adel Hicklin

Separator.

17

Sweet Springs Creamery. Picture taken in 2002.

in Sweet Springs. It was fun to go to the mill with him to buy feed, to the bank, and to the spring to get a gallon of sulphur water to drink. Then coming home he would stop at Kroneke's filling station and buy me an ice cream cone — my favorite was Tutti-Frutti.

Brownsville became Sweet Springs (pop. 1,628) in 1887 after a minister's ailing wife drank the spring water and recuperated.

Dad loved to fish. He fished in Crooked Creek on our farm and

Sweet Springs produce house. Picture taken in 2002.

other places. Mildred liked to fish also, and she went with Dad a lot. Sometimes we went to the cutoff, a backup from a creek or river, north of Marshall about five miles, with relatives and neighbors. The men would seine for fish, then we would have a big fish fry and picnic at Van Meter Park, halfway between Marshall and Miami, Missouri. Mary got a fishbone caught in her throat one time; she didn't eat much fish after that. After the picnic the fish were divided between the families and everyone went home tired and happy.

I used to go to Sedalia with Mom and Dad to shop. There was no heater in the car so we would wrap up in blankets to keep warm. Dad would have to scrape ice off the windows every so often. After shopping, Mom would hide Christmas gifts in shopping bags behind a curtain, behind the bed in the boys' room. There was no peeking. I liked to go shopping at Fisher's dime store in Sweet Springs on Christmas eve. That is where I bought the two blue bud vases for Mom, that I have now. They cost a whole ten cents each and they are very pretty.

The neighbors would come over to help on butchering day. Hogs would be scalded in a big vat over a fire under our mulberry tree on the other side of the garage, then hung in a tree where the hair was scraped off. They were then laid on tables that had been set up under the tree and were cut up and sausage was made and stuffed. Mom canned the tenderloin; the hams, shoulders and bacon were seasoned with brown sugar, salt, black pepper and red pepper (sugar cured) and hung in the smokehouse to cure. Lard was made from the fat in the big iron kettle over a fire until the cracklings were good and brown and no moisture left.

Mom always had spirea bushes and lots of flowers, honeysuckle vines, morning glories, roses, climbing roses, sweet peas, larkspur, cockscomb, zinnias and marigolds. Hollyhocks bloomed down by the pig pens, and they were pretty too. There were always humming birds around the honeysuckle flowers, and we could see their nests in the trees.

Some of the events that happened during my childhood:

1927 Charles Lindberg flew solo nonstop across the Atlantic Ocean.

Babe Ruth hit 60 home runs.

1928 Chillicothe, Missouri was the first place in the world to sell sliced bread.

1929 The stock market crashed October 24th.

1932 The Union Station Massacre, Kansas City, Mo.

Charles Lindberg's baby was kidnapped. I was five years old and I remember hearing about it and being afraid I would be kidnapped. Didn't matter that we had neither fame nor fortune, I thought my life was surely in danger.

1933 The average wage was 60% less than in 1929 and unemployment was 25%.

The Dionne Quints were born. I read everything written about them in the magazines.

The Star Spangled Banner was chosen as the national anthem.

The Empire State Building and Golden Gate Bridge were built.

1934-1936 — The dust storms forced many farmers over several states to give up their land.

1935 Will Rogers and Wiley Post were killed in a plane crash. Will Rogers was a favorite of my Dad's. He had a plaque in the garage with a quote of Rogers. It read "I never met a man I didn't like." That quote fit my dad perfectly.

1937 Amelia Earhart's plane was lost as she flew alone across the Atlantic Ocean, 22,000 miles into her scheduled 29,000-mile trip, near Howland Island in the Pacific Ocean.

The National Corn husking contest, to judge the best cornhusker in America was held in Marshall, Missouri. 100,000 people showed up. Mary's friend, Virginia Dennis, was the corn husking queen. So many bushels were picked by hand in so many minutes. A big event for Marshall that had a population of only 8,000.

Jim the Wonder Dog died in Marshall, Missouri. I had seen him at the Ruff Hotel in Marshall where he lived with his owner. Mom and Dad had seen him locate cars by a license number written on a card, and pick out a lady with a certain color dress. He would put his paw on the lady. He did many other things that were truly amazing. June Grimes (who later became my sister Mary's husband) was working at a funeral home in Marshall when Jim died. He embalmed him and put him in the baby casket that he was buried in. He was buried just outside Ridge Park Cemetery in Marshall, Missouri. The cemetery has grown, and his grave (always decorated) is now inside the cemetery and is surrounded by other graves. A memorial garden has been built just off the Square in Marshall, Missouri where the Ruff Hotel used to stand to commemorate Jim. Jim the Wonder Dog was a black and white setter born in 1925 from top performers. He was the runt of a litter and as a joke was sent to Van Arsdale, a hunter that traveled North America, who later claimed 5,000 quail were shot over Jim. Jim could predict the outcome of sporting events or elections, even understood foreign languages.

1938 Douglas "Wrong Way Corrigan" became a hero when he "mistakenly" flew solo across the Atlantic Ocean after U.S. Officials had forbidden the flight. He told them he would fly back to California, but instead landed in Ireland July

Jim the Wonder Dog (left) / Photo courtesy Joan Gilbert; The park in Marshall that preserves the legend of Jim is a curious stop in Marshall. / E. Counts photo.

21

18, 1938, 28 hours and 3,150 miles after he left New York. "My compass froze," he said. "I guess I flew the wrong way." He stuck with that story all his life.

Gypsies and salesmen of all kinds would come by our house. Mom always gave the gypsies something to eat (that was after they had already helped themselves to roasting ears from the field by the road). She bought vanilla, horse liniment and Petro Carbo Salve from the Watkins man.

I grew up in the Shirley Temple era, cutting out paper dolls and clothes of hers from magazines. I went to some of her movies and tried to tap dance like she did in the barn loft. I dreamed of having a Shirley Temple doll.

The Christmas of 1937 when I was 10 years old, all I wanted for Christmas was an autograph book. I was so disappointed when I woke up Christmas morning and there was nothing resembling it under the tree. Later John (my brother) and his wife, Ellen, arrived, and when I opened my package from them there was my autograph book with a matching diary. I still have the autograph book, and I treasure it because my dad, Mary, Rose, Mildred, Ellen and Elsie, among others, had written in it. Here is what my Dad wrote:

Christmas Day 1937

Any little gift that I could bring to you would be so small that it would be pathetic. So I bring you a gift of Love, a love that knows no time or space, a love that is stamped more indelibly upon my mind and heart than if it were carved in marble or in bronze, a love as limitless as space, and more enduring than eternity. I bring you The Christmas Spirit

Dad to Helen

Christian Union Church.

Mom and Dad and all of us went to Sunday school and church at Christian Union Church — a country church about three miles from our home — every Sunday. After we were ready to go, we would sit on or around the table until time to go. Dad taught a class and was an Elder. The men sat on one side of the church and the women on the other. Mrs. Hook played the piano and we all enjoyed singing the hymns.

Mom always had a crowd for dinner after church; usually the preacher would come home with us to eat and visit. In the afternoon sometimes we would play baseball in the driveway, and the preacher would play with us, or we would play croquet, horseshoes, or hide-and-seek. Sometimes I went home with a friend after church, but Mom would always save me a drumstick if they had chicken for dinner. I always knew where to look for it. It would be under the tea towels in a drawer of the kitchen cabinet. There was never any field work on Sunday, but chores always had to be done.

***Helen Elizabeth
at age 10.***

There were ice cream socials at church with the ladies and men bringing homemade cakes, freezers of homemade ice

23

Rev. Crockett.

cream and big tanks of ice to cool soda pop. My favorite was crème soda. They put up a stage for entertainment. One year Shirley Waisner and I sang several songs. I don't know how entertaining it was, but it was a lot of fun. There were also basket dinners with a lot of long tables full of good food.

In the good old hot summertime we had two weeks of church meetings every night. During a long dry period one night we sang *Showers of Blessings* and before we got home it rained so hard on the dirt roads that we slipped and slid from side to side in the old Model T Ford coming down the big hill to our house. But everyone was happy, and it made a true believer out of me! I was baptized in a pond on Johnson's farm when I was 11 or 12 years old. There were also baptisms held on our farm in our big stock tank.

Some of the preachers I remember are: Rev. I.J. Kenney, who served the longest period of time, from 1907 to 1934; Rev. Ira Griffiths, the walking preacher from Nelson, Missouri; and Rev. James Crockett from Warrensburg, Missouri. The first communion cup used at Christian Union was a glass goblet given by Mrs.

Blondie and Baby Dumpling. Mildred and Helen at barn.

Helen, Eleanor Scott, pet chicken, kitten in front of separator house.   *Helen and pet chicken, 1936.*

William Treece, my great grandmother. Later preachers were Rev. Bryan Banta and Rev. Roy Rutherford.

We had a canary named "Dickie." He would get out of his cage sometimes when we were cleaning it and putting fresh papers in the bottom. We had to retrieve him from the roof a few times, and once from the big elm tree by the road. A neighbor graciously climbed the tree to get him. The last time he got out of his cage he flew into a mirror and killed himself. We fed him French's bird seed and bird biscuits. Mom would give him red hot peppers that he liked to eat. I handled one of the peppers one day, then rubbed my eyes. They burned for a long time and I remember Mom comforting me.

We always had dogs, cats and kittens on the farm. The cats stayed at the barn or by the separator house where they were sure to get some milk. Sometimes they would get milk squirted in their mouths when milking was being done, and they had a pan for milk by the separator house. I don't remember old Sue, but she was a special dog of my brothers and sisters and took care of them. I do remember Lindy, a hunting dog, that was our next dog. Later we had a dog named McArthur in honor of Gen. Douglas McArthur of World War II. Then we had Butch, Goldie and Tuffy. We had a cow named Blondie, and her calf was named Baby Dumpling. I

Mary, Helen, McArthur.

had pet chickens and a banty rooster that I ground corn for in an old coffee grinder.

When calves or pigs were born in the winter, Dad would bring them inside by the kitchen stove to warm them. They were fascinating little creatures, especially the pigs. It was fun to see them.

Important places to me were Christian Union Church, Herndon Store, Cretcher Store, Sweet Springs Dime Store and Kroneke's Service Station. At Cretcher Store we could get old-fashioned peanut butter bought in the bulk. It would be ladled into a cardboard carton while stirring to keep the oil from separating.

We had a radio with a big speaker, and we would listen to *Amos and Andy* and *Fibber McGee and Molly.* Then there was the Victrola we had to turn the handle to wind up. It played the few records we had, like *Music Goes Round and Round* and *In Your Easter Bonnet.*

Sitting on our front porch in the evening, we could hear the preaching at Antioch Baptist Church, about a mile away, during their summer meetings. We watched it rain, thunderstorm, saw rainbows and sunsets from there. A good place to hull peas (I didn't like to hull peas), snap green beans and many other things. Lots and lots of family and friends, even boyfriends, visited on our front porch. I loved that porch.

Cars had running boards at that time and we would take turns standing up and riding there. Francis had a car with a rumble seat — now that was neat! John and Joe probably had one, but I only remember Francis'. I think that attracted a lot of girls.

For our Christmas tree Dad would cut and bring in a cedar tree from the woods. We always made a star for the tree top out of cardboard covered with aluminum. We had fun decorating it by stringing popcorn — we had a long-handled popcorn popper —

Antioch Church.

and making construction paper chains. There were always gag gifts under the tree, like a pig's tail wrapped up, and other things. Crackerjacks were a special treat, with a prize in every box; and always a sack of hard candy and an orange for everyone. Mom made lots of candy, caramel popcorn balls, fruit cakes and a great Christmas dinner.

On a little table in the kitchen was a water bucket with a dipper that we all drank out of. The water had to be brought from the deep well on the other side of the barn. There was a rusty can hanging at the well that we drank out of there. The windmill was at this well and Dad filled the stock tank with that water.

In the spring there was an incubator in the boys' room. The boys were all gone from home by that time. Mom would put the eggs in it and hatch baby chickens, then they were moved to the brooder house with a heater to keep them warm when they were a few days old. They were soft and cuddly and nice to hold and put up to your cheek, and fun to watch eating and drinking water.

It was so neat seeing the golden wheat blowing in the breeze, the green corn fields, the pastures with horses and cattle grazing; even the hogs and pigs in their pens had their own special charm.

At Thanksgiving time we would buy a turkey from a neighbor

to have for Thanksgiving dinner. Mary made such a pet of one that no one could bear to kill it when Thanksgiving day came around.

Dad used to pour coffee in a pan, pour water on it and let it boil. It must have been really strong, but it smelled so good. He liked to hunt mushrooms after a spring rain. He would come back to the house with a hatful and Mom would fry them. I loved to hear him coming in singing *My Wild Irish Rose* that he sang to Mom, and *You are My Sunshine*. It was also nice to hear him whistling.

One of the first movies I remember seeing was *Gone with the Wind*. I also saw *Wizard of Oz* that came out in 1939, and, of course, the Shirley Temple movies. I saw them at the Sweet Springs theater.

There were a lot of family reunions at our house. Aunts, uncles, cousins and whoever else might show up, and reunions at Aunt Nell and Uncle Roy Crowder's, and at Aunt Mae and Uncle Luther Treece's.

In wintertime the neighbors would come to our house to play cards. Dad liked to play pitch and also played checkers and dominos. We had a board with pockets in the corners that we played carom (I think it was called) with checkers, shooting them into the pockets.

We went to the Sedalia State Fair every year, the boys having livestock to show and the girls having embroidery work, cakes or 4-H Club exhibits. Mom would have a big picnic lunch fixed: fried chicken, potato salad, deviled eggs, sliced tomatoes, cucumbers and other goodies. And, of course, ice tea and lemonade. At noon

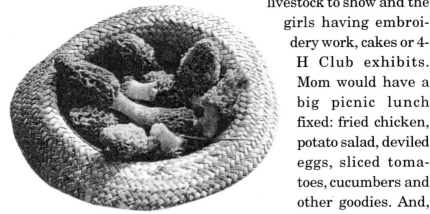

Hatful of mushrooms.

28

Family and friends in front of front porch. In front: Barbara Kueker, Phyliss Perkins. Front row: Rev. Banta, Amos Perkins, Leroy Treece (Dad), Uncle Roy Crowder, Uncle Luther Treece.

she would spread a big red and white checked tablecloth on the ground under a shade tree. We would all enjoy the meal, then go back for more fun at the fair.

Part of a family reunion. Visible in back row: Nell Treece (Mom), Helen Treece (my cousin's wife), Aunt Nell Crowder, Aunt Mae Treece, Rose Nell Treece, Ruth Jones, Mildred Treece. Front row: Barbara Kueker, Nancy Jones, Mary Treece, Phyliss Perkins.

Steps in front of Grandpa's house. Picture taken in 1996.

We also went to fall festivals, county fairs, carnivals, and to a circus that was set up under a big tent in Marshall. On July 4th we went to Sweet Springs to watch the fireworks display over the lake.

We had a big upright piano, and Dad took me to Sweet Springs once a week for my lessons for a few years.

Marshall had a man named Santa Claus. He got thousands of letters from children. "Santa" would write them all, enclosing a "check" with his autograph that said, "To the Bearer I offer 365 days of goodwill, good luck and happiness." In 1937 actress Mae West saw a story about how he was nearly broke, and she sent him $250 to buy postage stamps. He appeared in *Ripley's Believe It or Not.*

My Grandfather Joseph Sidney Treece was so tall, I remember being afraid of him, and would hide under the bed when he came to visit. I was only three years old when he died in 1930. My dad's mother, Laura, died when he was three years old in 1889. Grandfather remarried, and his wife, Eva, was just like a mother to my dad, his brother Luther and his sister Nell. Eva died in 1923 before I was born. Grandfather had a two-story house in Sweet Springs on Daisy Street (925, I think). There was a croquet play area beside the house. His name, J.S. Treece, is still carved in cement steps in front of the house near the street.

We visited Grandma Mary Alice and Grandpa George Henry Gregg in Independence, always taking a lunch to eat on the way. Grandma was a relative of Harry S. Truman, and my mother had seen him and Jesse James both get a spanking. It must have helped Harry but didn't do much for Jesse. Jesse's parents had probably come to Grandpa's to buy produce. When we arrived at their home, Grandma would have on a gray dress and gray apron, and she would be digging dandelions in the front yard and watching for us. Grandpa would be in his overalls. He worked at the Mt. Wash-

Laura Otilia Treece (Dad's mother).

ington Cemetery for many years beautifying the grounds. He died in 1935 when I was eight years old. Grandma died in 1950 when I was 23. Their house had an upstairs with two bedrooms. Downstairs there was a dark living room, a bedroom, big dining room and an old kitchen. There was a garage, an outhouse, a shed and a cellar. Grandma always had a canary. She would cover the cage when she wanted him to be quiet. Grandpa had a large truck garden and he sold produce. When my mom was young, she would take horse and wagon loaded with produce to the Kansas City market before daybreak.

Mildred wrote, "Mom and all of us got up very early and shocked wheat the day we went to Grandpa Gregg's funeral. Either that day or another something went wrong with the car. Dad picked out a new automobile, and we traveled on in style to Independence."

I don't remember much about my oldest brother, John, being at home, just that he was always going and coming in his car,

Back row: Aunt Mae and Uncle Luther Treece, Aunt Nell and Uncle Roy Crowder. Center row: Virginia Crowder, Bill Treece, Louise Crowder. Front row: Grandma (Eva Virginia) and Grandpa (Joseph Sidney Treece, Dad (Leroy Joseph) and Mom (Nellie Lee Treece). In front: Leonard Treece, John Treece, Joseph Treece.

always working someplace. He and Ellen Barger were married in Polo, Missouri, October 14, 1933, when I was six years old. He and Ellen would come to visit and play cards. Ellen was an elementary school teacher, and at that time a woman couldn't teach if she was married. Therefore, they kept their marriage a secret until 1938. She was one of my teachers in grade school. I went to stay a week with John and Ellen when they lived close to Herndon School, about one and a half miles away, and I got terribly homesick.

John told about the time he tried to get work at the Ford Plant in Kansas City. He stood in line for weeks at a time with feet wrapped in newspapers inside his shoes to keep his feet warm. He never did get hired. He milked and delivered milk for

Henry Fisher Dairy his last year in high school, worked for Uncle Roy Crowder one year on the farm; his pay was $22.50 per month. The next two years he worked in various places. Either just before or right after working for Uncle Roy was when he tried to get work at the Ford Plant. He shocked corn in the fall, and two or three summers he ran the tractor and was engineer on John Roscher's threshing crew. They did a lot of threshing in the Malta Bend area. They had a cook shack, and slept mostly on straw piles or in barns if it was raining. John also drove a stock truck to St. Louis part-time. Later he

Grandma
(Mary Alice Gregg).

rented a farm south of Blackwater, and had 175 acres of corn planted, working day and night. It was a very hot and dry summer and the corn burned up. He then started farming on the Ruth place, which joined Herndon School on the east side. In the spring of 1940 he moved to a farm three miles north of Sweet Springs.

Grandpa Gregg in his garden.

My mom and dad were such very special people. They had a deep love for each other, all their children, and all others. Never saying a bad word about anyone, always finding the good in people. They were our inspiration and always set a good example for us to follow. When my dad was asked which one of us he

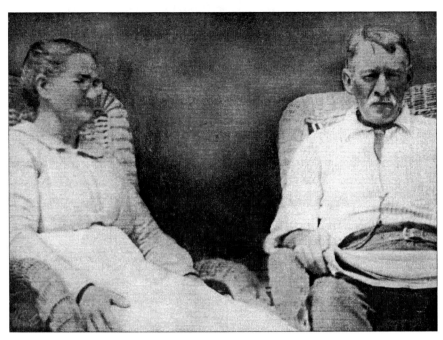

Grandma and Grandpa Gregg, 1924.

Mom and her brother and sisters. Aunt Georgia Poindexter, Mom, Aunt Leola Gilmore, Uncle Everett Gregg, Aunt Mayme Drummond, Grandmother Mary Alice Gregg.

liked the best his reply was, "The one that needs me the most at the time." My mother's family was of Irish descent and my father's was English.

While writing this, I realized even more that I was a witness to all of this, but I never had to do the hard work that my brothers and sisters did. I know they loved me anyway, and I loved and respected all of them and Mother and Father with all my heart.

In 1933, when Franklin Delano Roosevelt came into office, he vowed to ease the Great Depression. Overproduction was ruining farm prices so he paid the farmers not to raise corn and hogs and to kill off extra cows.

John and Ellen.

1938-39

Students of Herndon School pose for a group photo. Pictured are: (first row) Virginia Craighead, James Ludgan, Helen Howe, Charles Aulgur. Second row: Oscar Canida, Edward Willig, Wilma Jean Crawford, Cecil Aulgur, Doris Blackerly , Edward Herndon, Donald Scott. Third row: Eugene Craighead, Bill Howe, Ethel Dillion, Eleanor Scott Aulgur, Velma Canida, Helen Treece, Shirley Wasiner, Clarance Blackerly, Charles Fulkerson, Alford Crawford. The teacher was Miss Ellen Barger. (Photo courtesy of Eleanor Scott Aulgur)

Mom and Dad.

Cowboy sage Will Rogers was quoted as saying, "Roosevelt's New Deal is where a man has two cows, the government buys them both, shoots one, milks the other and throws the milk away."

II

School Days

SCHOOL DAYS — I went my first eight grades to Herndon School in a one-room school, with one teacher. The teacher would arrive early to start the fire in the coal-burning stove at the back of the room to have the room fairly warm by the time the students arrived. On the coldest days my dad was always there early to be sure it was warm. There were two outhouses, one for the boys and one for the girls. There were a few students in each grade. We had individual desks (with inkwells) that were attached to the seat. We walked one mile to and from school, which started at 8 a.m.

Ready to go to school. Back row: Margie Roscher, Mary, Mildred. Front row: Helen, Eleanor Scott.

Herndon School.

and let out at 4 p.m., with one hour for lunch at noon. It was a real treat for me if Mom and Dad had been to Sedalia shopping and would stop by school on their way back and give me a ride home.

I hated wearing the long underwear that was necessary to keep warm. I had to fold the legs over at the ankles and pull long brown or tan socks over them; they were secured above the knee with elastic garters. Sometimes in the springtime I would take the underwear off and hide them under the mattress before going to

The whole school — Grades 1 through 8. That's Helen, back row on right side.

School desks with inkwells.

school. After a big snow we would walk on snow drifts by the side of the road going to school. Discipline was quick, certain and painful if you got out of line in school. I made sure I didn't get into too much trouble. Punishment was by a wooden paddle with holes in the wood. If you missed a spelling word, you stayed after school and wrote the word 100 times on the blackboard.

There was a persimmon tree between home and school. On the way home from school in the fall we would pick some to eat. On the inside of the seed would be the shape of a spoon or fork; whichever you got meant something, but I have forgotten what. Sometimes you would bite into a bitter persimmon that would pucker your mouth; when they were dead ripe, they were sweet and good.

I wore dresses that Mom made to grade school. Sometimes Aunt Leola would bring Mom some fancy buttons to use. I remember one dress that had buttons shaped like parrots and had pretty colors. I thought that was something really special.

My teachers were Alice Giese, Betty O'Dell (she had an Austin car), Ellen Barger Treece, Virginia Rehkop and Miss Jennings. Mrs. Rehkop lived in Blackburn, Missouri. Shirley Waisner and I

7th Grade, 1940. Helen and Mrs. Virginia Rehkop.

went home with her a couple of times and stayed all night. She and her husband lived on a farm; it was always fun going there.

My favorite subjects in grade school were arithmetic, science and an agriculture class. I've forgotten what it was called, but we studied chickens, cattle, horses, etc. I made scrapbooks with construction paper for the back and front, with fancy lettering copied from a magazine *(The Saturday Evening Post)* and cut out for the title one color paper on top another color underneath, and pictures cut from magazines to go with the stories inside. If English had been my favorite subject, I could (maybe) have written a better book.

Making scrapbooks stayed with me and I have made many, many, many over the years, plus some for our children and grandchildren. I guess this book, as well as the one I edited for Ray titled *My Three Years in the Marine Corps,* is sort of a scrapbook with all the pictures. I loved doing it.

We had Halloween and Valentine's Day parties at school, and Christmas plays at school and church that we took part in. Those were always special times and a lot of fun. One morning after Halloween when we arrived at school there was a farm wagon, some other machinery and an outhouse on the porch. I think my brother Francis may have had a part in that prank. Valentine's Day was my favorite day of the whole year. Everyone exchanged valentines, and we took a decorated box to school to put our valentines in.

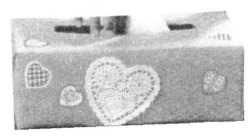

Valentine box.

Box suppers were held to raise money for some project at school. Each person decorated a box and fixed a good lunch to put in it. The boxes were then auctioned off to the highest bidder and you would get to eat the lunch with whoever bought your box.

My nickname in grade school was "Tootsie." Dad had given me that name. Eleanor Scott was "Scotty," Velma Canida was "Katy," and Shirley Waisner was

Eleanor Scott.

"Opsis." Eleanor rode "Lady," her pony, to school. I never liked to ride the horses at home because they were so big, but I did like to ride Lady. Eleanor and I used to visit in each other's homes and spend the night. Shirley and I used to do that also.

Recesses at school were spent playing baseball, practicing high jump, broad jump, relay races, or jumping rope with one person on each end of the rope and two jumping in the middle. We played

Shirley Waisner.

Andy-Over, Fox and Goose, London Bridge, Farmer in the Dell, Drop the Handkerchief, Follow the Leader, Tug-of-War, just horsed around, or ran down the road by the school, then running back

Eleanor Scott, Helen Treece, Velma Canida, at Eleanor's home.

School bell.

before the bell rang.

We took our lunch to school and ate outside if the weather was nice. Of course, we enjoyed the last day of school best. We had a picnic, played baseball, had running and jumping contests. I wasn't very good at baseball, and was usually the last one picked when they were choosing up sides, which was terribly embarrassing. But I excelled in broad jump and high jump. Of course, I didn't have much competition. We had a teeter-totter at school and one at home.

We got our lessons by kerosene oil lamps, later by Aladdin lamps. The lamps had to be kept filled and the globes washed.

We had a lot of big snows in winters and did a lot of sledding. Roschers, who lived across the road from us, had a big hill for a driveway that was good sledding; also a big hill on past Herndon Store that was great. There wasn't enough traffic to worry about.

Joe, Francis and Mary used to like to ride the horses at home.

1940. 7th grade, last day of school. Eleanor Scott, Helen Treece, Shirley Waisner.

Joe and Francis would ride them when the creek was up and make them swim from one end to the other. Joe remembered hitching the horses, "Maude" and "Becky," to the buggy and it turned over crossing the creek. He didn't remember how many were in or on it, but Joe had a scar on his elbow from the accident. Mary and her friends liked to ride together. When they would get over the hill, they would ride

Margie Roscher.

fast thinking Dad wouldn't know, but he always did and he would scold her for it. Mary said if anyone fell off "Maude" she would stand still and not step on them.

Joe remembered Grandpa Treece coming to the farm with horse and buggy. I can remember my great uncle Wade Treece coming to our house. He had tuberculosis and Mom would scrub, clean and disinfect everything when he left.

Margie Roscher and I were great pals, and she gave me the nickname "Teddy." She lived across the road from us, and we spent a lot of time together. A lot of it sitting on the bank, or in the swing waiting for Clyde, the mailman. I liked to order samples of cosmetics and things that were advertised in magazines, and I liked to cut out paper dolls and clothes from the magazines. There was a big elm tree close to the mailbox, also a big lilac bush. On the bank Mildred had buried her pet rabbit and put up a wooden marker. When the telephone repair man came to fix the lines, he wanted to know who was buried there.

We also enjoyed sitting under our big hickory nut tree on the hill, fishing from

Mailboxes.

a bridge on the road (there's no way any fish could have been there), and swimming in Roschers' pond that was about one-half mile back of their house. I didn't know how to swim and I stepped in a deep hole; that was about it for me. Margie pulled me out the third time I came to the top. That was the end of the pond swimming for me. On Margie's graduation card that she gave to me, she wrote, "I shall remember you as the pest who lived next door."

Margie, Mildred and I would walk across the fields back of Roschers' house to my Aunt May's. She had an old pump organ that we liked to play. Aunt May liked to curl my hair with a curing iron. The iron had to hang in the globe of a lamp to heat and had to be reheated often. One time when we wanted to go to see Aunt May and Uncle Luther I had a boil on my leg and couldn't walk so Mildred and Margie carried me.

It was always fun going to see Louise (my cousin) and husband Amos. Louise always made very good bread, butter and brown sugar sandwiches.

Mildred and I liked to go to Aunt Nell and Uncle Roy's. They lived next to the Cretcher Store and were the only ones in the neighborhood with indoor plumbing. I remember going up in their attic where they had sliced apples laid out on towels to dry. Funny what a person remembers. Our second cousins, Leroy Kueker and Monroe Perkins would sometimes be there.

We stayed a week with Aunt Leola Gilmore in Kansas City one summer. She took us to Fairyland Park and to some stage shows and movies.

I went to 4-H Club in the summertime. I belonged for several years and learned to sew.

Cretcher Store. January 1975, just before it was torn down.

44

Aunt Leola Gilmore, 1942, on Beautiful Lady.

I made a lot of gathered skirts, blouses and pajamas. 4-H Camp was held at Knob Noster, Missouri for a week, — we stayed in cabins in the woods, had a lot of fun, and sang a lot in our cabin at night. We sounded pretty good out in the woods.

I remember Joe and Francis hunting rabbits. They would come back from hunting with big bunches of them and then take them to town to sell. Joe used to tell about him and John going hunting and trapping. The first skunk they caught with their dog Sue they took to the house alive in a gunny sack to show Dad. They were excited about it and called Dad to "come and see what we got." Dad told them to "get that thing out of here."

In the good old hot summertime Joe saw a neighbor boy plowing without his shirt on, so he thought he could do that, too. What a terrible sunburn he had!

Our cousins Kenneth and Alice Drummond used to come from Kansas City to visit and stay a week or two. Kenneth was Francis' age and Alice was Mary's age. The boys were always playing tricks on the girls and getting into trouble.

We stayed in Sweet Springs one winter in Grandpa Treeces's house so the boys could go to high school. One evening Mom prepared the meal for John and Joe's vocational class.

Helen (in gathered skirt I made) and Mary.

45

Everything always seemed to happen to Joe. He was riding a motorcycle with Kenneth Leonard when he hit a rough spot in the road that left Joe sliding there on the seat of his pants — "as long as they lasted," Joe said — "then guess what." Francis and Howard Akeman bought a motorcycle, and Joe had a few misfortunes on that one also, especially riding it in the clover field.

Alice Drummond.

After high school Joe and Francis would walk to Sweet Springs every morning for some time in hopes of getting a job at the shoe factory. They didn't get on for a while, but both worked there later.

Sometime along the way we acquired an icebox to use instead of cooling food in the cellar. It had a place for a block of ice that Dad would go to the ice plant in Sweet Springs to get. He would wrap it in newspaper to keep it from melting too much on the way home. It worked just a little bit better than the cellar.

Joe and Elsie Thomas were married July 9, 1938 at the parsonage of Rev. James A. Crockett in Warrensburg, Missouri. I was 11 years old. Mildred and I stayed a week with them when they lived in Sweet Springs and they were both working at the shoe factory. I remember picking peas in their garden and their house being neat and pretty with lots of sunshine.

I remember Francis dating a lot of different girls. He had a Ford coupe with a rumble seat. We all liked to ride in that. He worked in California for a while in a CCC (Civilian Conservation Corps) camp. One of many programs that F.D.R. (Franklin Delano Roosevelt) set up to put young men to work who were out of a job. Francis told of seeing an octopus by the ocean.

Francis was married to Fay King August 30, 1940 at the Kings' home, by Rev. Ira Griffiths. I was 13 years old.

Mary was eight years older than I. There were dances in people's homes at that time, also barn dances. We went as a family to some of the neighbors' dances, mostly square dancing. Dad

didn't like for Mary to go to the
barn dances, and I can remember her being **extremely** up-
set one time when he told her
she couldn't go. We had a big
flat boulder of rock that was
outside the window of the girls'
room. It was great to sit on and
it would seat three people.
Mary sat there for some time
thinking things over.

Ice box. Ice goes in top left.

Mary did a lot of sewing.
She made Rose some dresses
and a coat. Wonder how many dishes Rose had to wash! Mary
made an angel food cake almost every Saturday, using many eggs,
and made pink icing. I got to lick the pan. Saturdays were spent
baking pies, cakes, bread and churning butter for Sunday dinner.

Mary and I were good pals. One time she asked me to go to the
barn to ask Dad if she could go on a date. Dad told me, "If Mary
wants to go on a date she can ask me herself." Mary went on many
dates. She dated Charles Roscher for quite a while, then she met
June Grimes and Charles was history.

Mary took a commercial course at Mercy Academy in Marshall

Left: Joe and Elsie.

*Right: Francis and
Fay, 1940.*

June and Mary,
March 9, 1942,
in New Orleans, LA.

after high school, while staying at Langans doing housework to pay for her room and board. Langans owned a grocery store and later, during the war, they would save bananas for Mary and me. Mary worked at the A.S.C. (Agricultural Conservation Association of Saline County) from 1939 to 1943. In March of 1942 she went by train to New Orleans where June Grimes was stationed in the Army. They were married there March 9th. They kept their marriage a secret because she couldn't work in a government office if she was married. In 1943 Mary worked as a stenographer in the personnel department of Aircraft Accessories Cooperation. In 1944 for the Bureau of Census in Kansas City, Missouri. Later in 1945 as field representative for Production Credit Association in Marshall.

Rose was six years older than I. She was very smart and pretty, with very dark hair and eyes. I remember her going on dates and having a good time with her friends. She was the best in her class in typing and shorthand. A very special person, very sweet. She was only 19 years old when she died after a years illness with a menses problem; May 30, 1940. I'm quite sure with today's medical knowledge it would be something that could easily be treated and cured. I remember Dad coming outside to tell me, "Rose is not going to make it." I was 13 years old. Rose (Rose Nell) was named for the roses blooming outside Mom's window on November 1, 1920, when she was born, and for Mom, whose name was Nellie Lee. Mildred and Rose were especially close. Rose liked to embroider, and she gave Mom a set of embroidered tea towels for her birthday, March 17, 1940.

August 3, 1940 John Roger, my first nephew, was born to Ellen,

Rose Nell.

John's wife. Ellen died that same night from hemorrhaging. I remember the call Mom and Dad got that night after we had gone to bed, and the terrible shock of it. The year of 1940 was very sad indeed, especially on Rose's birthday and at Christmastime.

November 9, 1941 my first niece was born to Francis and Fay. She was named Joyce Alene. A beautiful little girl to love.

Mildred was four years older than I. She helped Dad a lot in the field, bringing in the cows and milking. We did a lot of things together, like going to 4-H Club, putting on shows in the barn hayloft, doing acrobat acts and tap dancing. We liked to sleigh ride, play jacks, marbles, dominos, checkers, tiddlywinks, spin tops, play tag, hopscotch, walk on stilts, and jump off the hen house roof. We had a tire swing and a wooden-seat swing and a chinning

John Roger Treece.

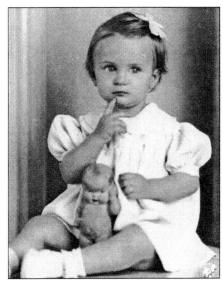

Joyce Alene Treece.

49

Mil and Ed, 1945.

bar. It was fun playing on a haystack or riding on a load of hay. The aroma of new-mown hay was delightful. Because Mildred liked to work outside, Dad gave her the nickname "Bill," and the rest of us called her that also.

Mildred's birthday and mine were a week apart, and when I was 14 years old Mom and Mary planned a surprise birthday party for both of us. It was a surprise and a lot of fun. All our young neighborhood friends were there. We played blind-man's-bluff, spin-the-bottle, post office and musical chairs. Mary had baked an angel food cake (of course) for our birthdays.

Mildred and Ed Armentrout were married in Sedalia, Missouri at the minister's home, August 24, 1941. They were shivareed at our home. They moved to Hartford, Connecticut where Ed was employed by United Aircraft of East Hartford.

My first permanent was by a huge contraption of a machine, and a bad experience. I was burnt on the back of my head and had a huge scab for a long time, but I'm sure I looked beautiful with all that frizz.

I don't know how old I was when I started to drive. Dad had a '33 or '34 Chevy. I asked him to take me to a girlfriend's house when he came in from the field one

Perm machine.

night. I guess he was tired so he told me if I wanted to go, to take the car and go. So I did. That is how I learned to drive. No licensing was required to drive at that time. When I did apply for my driver's license, they only asked how long I had been driving.

Mom had a lady seamstress close to Herndon to make Mary and me velvet dresses. Mary's was aqua and black, mine was maroon and gray, and they were made alike. Our children, Mary's daughter

Ad appeared Nov. 22, 1934

CHEVROLET
QUALITY

THE MASTER CHEVROLET $540 AND UP

1934 Chevy.

Terry and our daughter Debbie, later had fun using those as dressup dresses. The lady also made me a blue and gray wool pleated

Helen, Mildred, Mary, Fay, Francis, Elsie, Joe, Viola, John, Mom. (That's my gray and blue pleated wool skirt.)

skirt that I wore, wore and wore when in high school, and she made me a red chiffon long-sleeved blouse that I loved to wear. I wore it with a gray wool pleated skirt.

Helen and Ray (my velvet dress). 1942.   *Helen in gray pleated skirt.*

III

High School Days and WWII

I STARTED TO Marshall High School in 1941, riding the big yellow bus 13 miles to and from school. High school was a huge building compared to the one-room school I had been going to for eight years. I worried about getting from one class to the next on time, finding the classroom, being able to work the combination on my locker and a few other things. If the bus was early or I was running late, like the time I burnt a hole the shape of the iron in the blouse I was going to wear, Dad would take me to school, or come to Marshall to get me if I missed the bus to come home. Vesta Thomas and Eleanor Scott were my good friends.

December 7, 1941

I was ready to go to Sunday school, sitting on the floor reading the funny papers, when we heard on the radio that Japan had bombed Pearl Harbor. What I remembered at that time was that we had been selling scrap iron to Japan. A lot of people didn't even know where Pearl Harbor was. I was three months into my ninth grade on December 8, 1941 when we were called into assembly in the high school auditorium to listen to the declaration of

Vesta Thomas.

war. President Roosevelt declared war on Japan. The place was very quiet. I'm sure none of us realized what was to come. Four days later Germany and Italy declared war on the United States, and everything changed. The war started the year I entered high school and ended the year I graduated. All of us were greatly affected by the war. There were news reels before the movies started, telling the news of the war.

Four months after Pearl Harbor, on April 18, 1942, sixteen B25 Mitchell twin engine bombers were launched from the carrier U.S.S. Hornet. They bombed Yokahama and Tokyo. That was called "The Doolittle Raid."

Many people would go to 40 Highway near Sweet Springs, stand beside the highway and wave to the troops going by. We listened to Bob Hope, Fred Allen, Jack Benny and newsman H.V. Kaltenborn on the radio.

Rationing started in January of 1942 to conserve food and material for the war effort. You needed money and books of stamps to buy anything from sugar to shoes. The stamps were red, blue, brown or green, and each was worth a different number of points. If the item you wanted was available, and if you had enough points and money, you could buy it. New cars, large or small appliances, and most other things were not made. It wasn't hard to adjust to rationing, after growing up in the depression when almost everything was in short supply. To get your ration stamps you had to go to the local ration board to fill out lengthy forms. Most people got an A windshield sticker, which meant three gallons of gas per week. B was for a little more. Dad's was probably a C because of being on the farm. New tires were allocated according to priority, and to save wear and tear on tires there was a national speed limit of 35 mph. Needless to say, there was not much traffic.

Our family didn't have to worry about meat rationing since Dad had his own meat. Otherwise, the limit per week was two pounds, and that was for whatever meat the butcher was able to acquire.

Coffee grounds were used over and over and over until it was nothing but colored water. Bananas were used to make gasoline for war machines. Jell-O, chewing gum and films were not available. Occasionally, a store would get in a small amount and we could stand in line hoping they didn't run out of the item before you got to the end of the line. Companies changed over to making war-related items or were forced to close their doors.

Ray Merrell.

I guess my first date was with a boy who lived close to Herndon. I only went for a ride with him in his very neat red convertible. My dad didn't like that one bit, and he let me know it in no uncertain terms. He even threatened to send me to Sweet Springs High School instead of Marshall if I didn't quit seeing him. Which, of course, I did; it was no big deal anyway; and not to worry — he soon found a cute redhead.

In the spring of 1942 Margie Roscher and other friends started having parties at their homes. Margie had been going with Raymond Merrell, and he was her date for the party at her house. She had a piano and I played it at her party (probably showing off for someone I thought was pretty neat). The next time she had a party she asked me who I wanted her to ask to be my date. She was a good sport about it when I told her Raymond Merrell.

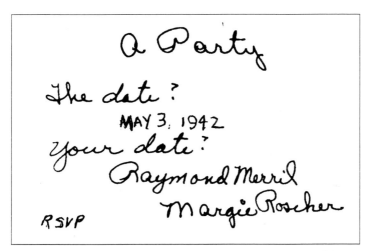

Invitation (she didn't spell his name correctly).

Ray Merrell, 1942.

That started a wonderful summer of dating. Mom and Dad liked Raymond from the start, and that was a big plus for me. Raymond didn't always have a car, so we double-dated with other couples, which got me into trouble later.

I guess he had a car, but it didn't always run. Before we started dating he had a white 1929 Model A convertible Ford. I had seen it in a ditch one morning when I was on the school bus. It had isinglass windows that could be snapped on in winter or when it rained. It had been slick the night before and he had slid into the ditch and folded a wheel under. He went to the junk yard the next day and bought a couple of wheels for fifty cents each. When we started dating he had a 1933 Hudson Essex Terraplane car, medium green with fenders that were painted pea green. Wow!

In June of 1942 John and Viola Scott were married at the Christian Church in Sweet Springs. It was a beautiful wedding and now we were all happy that Roger would have a real home.

Raymond and I went to the movies in Marshall and Sedalia, (one time we stopped at Herndon and called Mom and Dad to see if it was okay if we went to the midnight movie — it was okay), cel-

Helen and Ray.

ebrated the 4th of
July by throwing
fire crackers off a
bridge into flood wa-
ters in Sweet
Springs; we went to
carnivals, fall festi-
vals, and went to see
a train wreck in
Marshall, to Sedalia

Terraplane.

and Sweet Springs
to dances, and one Sunday afternoon he took me for a plane ride,
sightseeing over Marshall. I had on a white sharkskin skirt that I
had made — I don't know why I remember that—but I can remember getting into his car wearing it. One of the movies we went
to see was *The Pride of the Yankees,* the Lou Gehrig story, where
Gary Cooper spoke the words," Today I consider myself to be the
luckiest man on the face of the earth," and we sat in the balcony at
the Mary Lou Theater in Marshall. It was a very sad movie and I
cried. We went to a little restaurant in Marshall that had little
round tables and drugstore chairs. It was fun going there and we
liked to drink cherry Cokes or limeades.

We went to parties at friends' homes, and I had a party. One
Sunday we went to the bluff, close to Marshall Junction, with an-

Viola, John and Roger. Garage, barn and windmill in background.

Ray and Helen at the bluff.

other couple, and we climbed to the top. We took pictures with Mom and Dad's box camera. It was very windy.

Raymond would take different roads coming out to see me. There were many ways to get there, and he knew all of them.

Before starting to go to the parties we had seen each other around Marshall with different groups of kids at places like "The Spot," a little hamburger place, and at Louie Stedam's gas station (I just happened to walk by), where he would be working on his car. We saw each other at a carnival one night. We went somewhere with another couple in their car, and when we came back to the carnival someone had stolen his bicycle.

The best hot dogs we *ever ate* were at a little hole-in-the-wall place that specialized in hot dogs and chili dogs — five blocks north of the Bothwell Hotel on the west side of the street in Sedalia, Missouri. No air conditioning, of course, and the cook would line the buns up his sweaty arm (added flavor), added the hot dogs, onions and relishes or chili. We thought they were the best ever — they must have been, because we still remember them — or we wonder how we survived.

We were out with two other couples one night and they didn't want to go home as early as we did. We ended up getting home at 3:00 a.m., and that was not good! Luckily, Mom and Dad didn't know it was Raymond I was with. My dad said, "I don't know what bunch you were out with, but you're not going out with them again."

There was a big tent roller-skating rink at the edge of Marshall and we skated there a lot. We

Ray at the bluff.

58

liked to skate together in the Moonlight Skate. We also went skating at Carrollton after dropping by to see Ray's Grandmother and Grandfather Uhrig.

We had an old striking clock that would strike the moment you came in from a date, giving away the time. Then there was the telephone with six to eight others on the same line. When we got a call you could hear the other receivers coming off the hooks. That way everybody knew what everyone else was doing. Each person on the line had a certain ring, like three longs and

Our striking clock.

a short. We could ring anyone that was on the line, but if you wanted to call long distance you had to ring "central" and tell her the number and she would ring it.

I was staying in Marshall with Mary at the Marshall Apartments while going to high school in the fall. Raymond and I went to the high school and college football games. One night I went with some girlfriends, as Raymond and I had a little difference of opinion. He met me after the game and took me home but wouldn't let me go in until I promised to see him the next night; so I promised.

Mildred and Ed's baby girl, Dorothy Rose, was born November 17, 1942. She was named for our sister Rose who had died, and for Ed's sister Dorothy, who had died of polio. My second niece, and another beautiful girl to love.

November 25, 1942 Raymond enlisted in the U.S. Marines. He went from Sedalia by train to St. Louis, where he

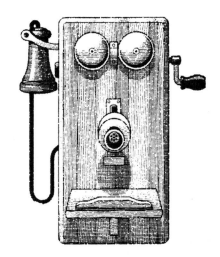

Wall telephone.

Marshall Apartments.

was given a physical and was issued a uniform to have his picture taken in. From St. Louis he rode the Union Pacific train line to San Diego. He remembers fondly stopping at the North Platte, Nebraska canteen where they were greeted and given sandwiches, other food, and something to drink. The people met every train

Mildred and Dotty, 1945.

that went through North Platte, day and night, and by the end of the war had given time and food to six million servicemen, using their own ration stamps to feed them, and gas rationing stamps to drive to the canteen. Bob Greene has written a very good book, *Once Upon a Town,* about the North Platte Canteen. The book is dedicated to Keith Blackledge, former editor of *The North Platte Daily Telegraph,* and his wife Mary Ann. Ray trained for three months at San Diego, Camp Elliott and Greens Farm; then was sent overseas to the South Pacific, and did not return until December 13, 1945. But that story is in his book *My Three Years in the Marine Corps.*

In January 1943 Raymond's sister and I became very good friends. We would tell each other when we got a letter from Raymond, walked uptown to eat lunch with each other, went to movies, and with our friend Mary Ruth (she had a car) we went to Slater to have our fortunes told, to Sedalia to skate or dance, or Sweet Springs to swim or picnic, that is whenever we could talk someone out of a gas stamp and save up our nickels, dimes and quarters. We thought we were rich if we could save up $2.00.

We also wrote **a lot** of long notes to each other in study hall and in our classes. Dotty taught me to ride a bike and I taught her to play piano. Dotty was recently home to Missouri from Colorado and she let me read her 1944 and 1945 diary and notes I had written her when we were in our sophomore and some in our junior year of high school. What a treasure after all these years — teenager's

Ray in Museum in North Platte, Nebraska. Display picture of troops being fed. Picture taken September 2002.

notes with all our planning — and *wise* sayings of the time.

On April 2, 1943, on New Caledonia, Raymond and Robert Lindsay joined the Marine Raiders and went into the 2nd Raider Battalion. Their first duty was to help build Camp Allard, named for Robert Allard, who was killed during the Makin Raid when he and four others attempted a rescue from their submarine back to the island.

V-mail was tried during the war to cut down on the weight on planes, but no one liked it. Letters were photocopied and made smaller, but lost the personal touch. We both wrote a few v-mail letters but went back to regular letters. V-mail wasn't required, only suggested. Sometimes Ray *had* to write v-mail as there was no other paper or envelopes available.

April 2, 1943 Dotty, Mary Ruth and I started to Marshall Junction. The gearshift went out of her car and we walked about a mile to the Junction to get someone to fix it.

In the summer of 1943 between my freshman and sophomore years, I stayed with John and Viola during the week when they lived in Mt. Leonard on a farm. I helped Viola cook for them and

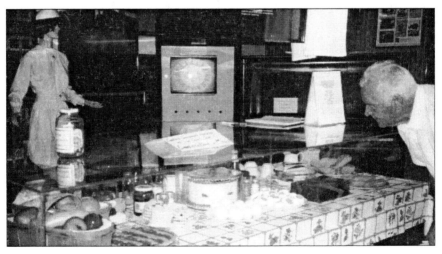

Canteen display in museum. Taken September 2002.

Site of the Union Pacific Railroad Depot containing famous WWII North Platte Canteen serving more than 6 million members of the Armed forces from December 25, 1941 to April 1, 1946. The canteen was supported by North Platte citizens and Nebraska and Colorado communities.

the farmhands. Ed Armentrout, Mildred's husband, also worked there and I rode back home with him on Friday evenings. He, Mildred and Dotty were back from Connecticut before Ed's going into the Navy in August of 1943.

One of the Burma Shave signs of the times read "Today's kids have missed a treat/moonlight rides in a rumble seat."

Raymond asked me in a letter to send him a code so he could let me and his folks know where he was. His letters were censored, but mine were not. I sent him a code and it worked pretty good.

November 1, 1943 Raymond, with the Marine Raiders, made the beachhead at Empress Augusta Bay, Bougainville. There were always newsreels before the movies. One time when Raymond's mother and dad went to the movies they were showing Marines being buried at sea; they walked out of the theater and didn't go back until the war was over and all three of their sons were home.

June Grimes, Mary's husband, was in the Army. Raymond was in the Marines and when Ed, Mildred's husband, joined the Navy, that made us the "Three Little Sisters." "One loved a soldier, one

Helen, Mary, Mil.
December 1945.

loved a sailor, and one loved a lad from the Marines." The Andrew sisters sang that song in the movie *Private Buckaroo.* There was also a movie of *Three Little Sisters.*

During the war Kate Smith, a tireless morale – booster, beautifully sang *God Bless America.* The U.S.O. was born, and the most popular bandleader, Glen Miller, was lost in the English Channel.

I stayed in Marshall sometimes with John, Viola and Roger. Their house had burned down from a spark on a dry shingle roof in Mt. Leonard, so they had moved to Marshall before moving to another farm. I also had an apartment with Dorothy Merrell and Vesta Thomas for a while.

In the winter of 1943 I had strep throat. Mom and Dad put me to bed and took good care of me. My throat was so sore I couldn't eat, and I lost 30 pounds.

My Saturdays were spent shampooing, getting my lessons, listening to the radio and writing to Raymond. I would write down

Mil, Ed, Helen,
Ray, Mary, June.
December 1945.

the names of the songs on the *Hit Parade* each week and send in his letter. I tried to write every day, and he wrote me as often as he could.

Everyone wanted to do as much as possible to help the war effort. We could never do enough. One thing we could do was to fold bandages at the courthouse for the Red Cross.

In high school we would go out on trucks to pick up scrap metal to be used in the war effort. Each class had their own pile that was piled high in the front area of the school, as high as we could pile it. There was a lot of competition between the classes. Scrap metal

Mary Ruth and Helen.

was picked up by the creek on our farm as well. One day we got out of school all day so we could gather milkweed pods. The pods were used to make life jackets. Some days we got out of school to work selling war bonds.

Occasionally we would see people lined up all the way down the street from some business, then you knew a store had gotten in some kind of merchandise that was in short supply, and you knew if you didn't need it someone else did, and you got in line with the rest hoping they wouldn't run out before you got there.

I attended Miss Mary Fisher's dramatics class and was in a couple of senior plays. I liked that class, and also shorthand, typing, bookkeeping and alge-

bra. I thought I wanted to be an algebra teacher — again, English wasn't one of my favorite classes — and I would get my shorthand lessons in American History class.

Some of us would walk uptown for lunch — our meeting place with other

Helen under a shade tree writing to Raymond.

Dorothy Merrell walking to work at Forum Cafeteria in Kansas City, MO.

friends uptown was at the Scott's Store — then run back to school so as not to be late for typing class. When it was cold, our hands were pretty stiff to type, but we struggled through. We had noisy typewriters with clattering keys, and I always liked to hear the bell ring each time you got to the end of a line. If a mistake was made, the paper was ripped out, wadded up and thrown away, more paper inserted and you started over. The ribbon had to be changed often, or straightened out if it got tangled.

I worked part-time at Missouri Valley Store in 1943 while going to school. It was like a department store; I worked downstairs in ladies accessories When a payment was made for an item downstairs the clerk put the cash or check in a small canister and pulled an overhead spring-loaded lever; it would streak to the cashier upstairs riding on two steel cables, one going and one coming. When the cashier finished with the transaction she pulled the lever and the basket came flying back with the change or a receipt for the sale.

I stayed with Mildred and Dotty south of the high school while I was working at Missouri Valley. One morning it was so cold, as I was walking to work I froze my nose. The skin of my nose would drip water, and it dripped, hurt and itched for days.

March 20, 1944

Raymond was on the Emirau invasion. There was no opposition, and they now called the Emirau operation Bloody Emirau.

In the summer of 1944 Dotty Merrell stayed in Kansas City with her sister Ernie and worked at the Forum Cafeteria. I stayed at 585 W. North in an apartment with Mary and worked at Cut-Price.

I took a Diversified Occupations class in high school, and from that I worked one-half day on school days and all day on Saturdays as assistant bookkeeper at Cut-Price Clothing Store, which was owned by Rose and Buckner. It was a men's shoe and clothing store. I later transferred to the Rose and Buckner store next-door. It was a men's clothing, and a shoe store for both men and women, and women's accessories. I worked full-time after graduation five days a week, eight to five, and Saturdays eight a.m. to nine p.m. My pay was $12.50 per week. I tried to buy one or two dollars worth of war stamps each week. According to my budget 22 cents went for withholding and Social Security tax. Some of the items bought during the month: airmail stamps were six cents each, birthday card, 26 cents; show and popcorn, 40 cents; coke was five cents; subscription to Life Magazine for Raymond, $3.75; supper, 35 cents; lipstick, $1.22; present for Dotty, 29 cents; cigars for Dad, 12 cents; bath powder for Mom, $1.22. During the month I paid Mary $10.00 on rent and $5.00 once in a while on groceries. I bought a magazine rack for Mildred and Ed for $6.07.

One night when I was living in the Marshall Apartments at 585 West North with Mary and got off work at 9 p.m., I was walking home and I thought someone was following me. I turned around to look and ran into a telephone pole. I ran the rest of the way home. I am quite sure if someone *was* following me there is no way he could have caught me. I also stayed with Mildred and Dotty at the apartments. Mrs. Sneerbush was the apartment manager. She was nosy, protective, and kept everyone in line. She babysat for Dotty when Mildred and Dotty lived at the apartments.

Anna Belle Halsey and I worked upstairs in the office at Rose and Buckners. We started getting our mail at the store, and when Benny Berg, the mailman, brought the mail, if I got a letter from Raymond or she got a letter from Charlie McGraw, he would yell upstairs to tell us we got a letter. If we were lucky, we both got a letter. We enjoyed working at the Rose and Buckner store.

Benny's brother was a shoe salesman at the store and when

he had a hearing impaired lady come in to buy shoes he would put on a big sales talk, telling her the shoes were made of Anna Belle hide, or Helen something or other. He had us embarrassed and laughing at the same time, and thinking — what if her hearing comes back!!

Lee.

After Mary left Marshall to work in Kansas City I kept the apartment for a while, then stayed with my sister Mildred and niece Dotty in their apartment before moving into a room in a house not far from the Rose and Buckner store with Cora Lea Merrell, Raymond's sister.

The owners of the store, the Roses and the Buckners, were very good to us. Mrs. Rose and her sister fixed up a really cute apartment upstairs in a building uptown. It was called the Uptown Apartments, and Anna Belle and I moved in there. I was living there when Raymond came home from the Marines, and I was still working at the store.

Working at the store the employees couldn't stand in line for nylon hose when they came in. Nylons (more sheer than silk but didn't sag, bag, or run quite so much), had replaced silk from Japan. What silk the U.S. had was being used for parachutes. The owners did give us one pair of nylons one year for Christmas. In 1942 all new nylon went to war, into tents and parachutes. Old nylons became gunpowder bags. With hose we wore garters or girdles. Panty hose were not made until 1959. In the meantime we used leg makeup that was supposed to look like hose, and since hose at that time had a seam up the back, we sometimes drew a line up the back of our legs with

Anna Belle and Helen in apartment.

Desk in Anna Belle and Helen's apartment. Ray Merrell and Charlie McGraw's pictures.

an eyebrow pencil. You can imagine how that looked. The stuff would come off on your clothes, so that didn't work out very good.

The O.P.A. (Office of Price Administration) sent out charts to stores, and we had to refigure the price of all merchandise, not going over the limit that was set. About the time we got it all figured out the limit would be changed and it would have to all be refigured.

While I was staying with Mary, we got homesick one Friday evening so we had the bright idea to walk out to Mom and Dad's, 13 miles, to the farm. We started out at dusk and it was soon dark. Not long after we got on the Herndon road a team of horses and wagon passed us and we were offered a ride. Later we wished we had said yes. No other traffic was on the road. We walked and walked. It was fun for a while, but by the time we got to Herndon we were very tired and cold and our feet so sore we didn't think we could walk any further. We called Dad from Herndon, two miles from home, to come get us. Mom fixed us hot tea and toast, heated some flat irons, wrapped them in newspapers to put at our feet in bed. Mom and Dad were always on call to take care of whatever.

Raymond sent me one dozen red roses for Easter 1944.

Helen, Ray, Anna Belle. December 1945.

Ray, Helen, Anna Belle.
December 1945.

They were beautiful and *One Dozen Roses* remains our favorite song.

April 5, 1944

Thomas Wayne was born to Joe and Elsie. Another great handsome boy. That makes me aunt four times. Two nephews and two nieces; and I'm sure there will be more to come.

We didn't see many young men around during the war. There were 38 boys in my graduating class and 62 girls. Some of the boys had already gone into the service. It was June 30, 1943 when Missouri Valley College was occupied by the V-12 (Navy Officers Training Corps). The Navy came to Marshall and there were many sailors around town.

Thomas Wayne Treece.

Raymond had been training on Guadalcanal for the attack on Guam. He landed on Guam July 21st, 1944, with the Fourth Marine Regimental Weapons Company, 1st Provisional Marine Brigade, for the recapture of United States Territory.

We had great music to lift our spirits during the war; big bands and big band singers. Ray's sister Mildred and I liked to skate to the tune of *Chattanooga Choo Choo.* A music selection on the jukebox was five cents. There was a skating rink upstairs in a building close to town where we skated.

We also had a teenage clubroom upstairs in another building on the square that some of us went to sometimes.
Songs on the Hit Parade July 20, 1944:

- *I'll Be seeing You*
- • *Swinging on a Star*
- *Long Ago and Far away*
- *Amore*
- *I'll Get By*
- *Goodnight Wherever You Are*
- *Sweet Loraine*
- *And Then You Kissed Me*
- *Milkman, Keep Those Bottles Quiet*
- *Dark Eyes*

— *This list provided by Dorothy Turner*

We could play our favorite songs from small jukeboxes attached to the booths in restaurants. Dotty and I liked to jitterbug wherever there was a dance floor.

In high school we still played baseball (ugh) on the back lot, but then we played volleyball and basketball, which I loved. I was captain of our team and won a letter. We played several small towns around Marshall. We had to wear ugly green baggy bloomer-like gym suits. We had a pretty redheaded gym teacher named Miss Rettig, and she was very nice. I finally got to be a better softball player and began to like it and was captain of the team.

I didn't like the showers at school, and one day while taking a shower someone stole my expansion bracelet that Raymond had given me, from my shower locker. The bracelet matched a heart-shaped locket necklace. I really didn't like the shower room after that.

Penny loafers, saddle oxfords (with white socks), pleated skirts and sweaters were popular; also rolled-up jeans — but not for school.

A.H. Bueker was principal and Hubert Wheeler was superintendent. I worked part-time in Mr. Wheeler's office. Mrs. Hilburn was our study hall teacher. She didn't have much control, as wit-

Hazel Leimkuler (Cindy).

*Mary Ruth Thomas
(Peachie).*

nessed by our passing notes, spending time out in the hall, sharpening our pencils so we could see what was going on outside or elsewhere in the room, or to pass notes, etc.

Helen Treece (Terry).

Dorothy Merrell (Dotty).

We had great assemblies. I can remember a boy from Slater singing *White Cliffs of Dover.* It was so good and so sad at the same time.

Our school colors were red and black, and our football team was the "Marshall Owls." Our pep song was written by our bandleader, Mr. Lickey. We had a great football team and a great band.

Mary Ruth Thomas, Dorothy Merrell, Hazel Leimkuler and I ran around together. Our nicknames were Peachie, Dotty, Cindy and Terry, and we called ourselves "The Four Belles." Mary Ruth had a car and lived on a farm so was able to get some gas and we went to Sedalia some. One night we were lost in Sedalia after going to Flat Creek Inn and we tried to turn around, but backed off into a ditch at a cemetery. There we were — stuck. Dottie and I walked to town to get a wrecker and Vesta and Mary Ruth stayed with the car. The wrecker came to pull us out but some soldiers had come by earlier and lifted the car out. The wrecker guy didn't charge us. Guess he figured we didn't have any money anyway.

June 6, 1943

Vesta and Dotty stayed all night with me. Mom and Dad took us to the movie in Sweet Springs to see *Casablanca.* They rode with me on the bus to the farm sometimes. The bus broke down many times and we would have to walk home from Herndon or Cretcher.

One time Dotty, Peachie, Cindy and I went to Carrollton with Dotty's mother, dad and Lee to her grandmother's house. We decided after lunch to walk uptown and go to a little restaurant, "The Vox," that had a dance floor. When Mr. and Mrs. Merrell got ready to go home they didn't know where we were and they had to get home to milk, so they left without us. There was no way for us to get home, so we started walking. There were very few cars traveling anywhere, but someone did stop and gave us a ride to Marshall.

October 28, 1944

Robert Joseph was born to John and Viola. Another handsome boy.

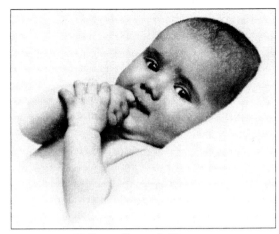

Robert Joseph Treece.

April 1, 1945

Easter Sunday, U.S. forces landed on Okinawa. Raymond with the 4th Marines 6th Marine Division made the beachhead at Yontan Airfield.

The following is a quote from Jerry Heaster of the *Kansas City Star:*

Okinawa — It is a serious historical injustice that the Battle of Okinawa has never received its due respect as probably the greatest combined land-air-sea campaign in the history of warfare.

The battle probably also was responsible for more deaths than any single action in Military history. Its importance has been overlooked though, because it was sandwiched between victory in Europe and the dropping of the atomic bombs that forced Japan's surrender.

Estimates of the death toll have always been in disagreement, but even the most conservative reckonings are awesome. The number of U.S. combatants who died has been estimated from 13,000 to 16,000.

Japanese military losses are put from 80,000 to 125,000 and estimates of Okinawan civilian dead range from 90,000 to 150,000.

And a quote from Joe R. Reider, Army Undersecretary:

For nearly three months, U.S. forces scratched their way across Okinawa's 60 miles of steep ridges, sheer cliffs, deep draws and slimy sucking mud. For the sailors off-shore it was day after day, night after night, wave after wave of terrifying kamikaze attacks that sank 36 ships and damaged another 368.

Okinawa cost 13,241 American lives, including 8,343 sailors, Coast Guardsmen and Marines, the highest single campaign toll in all Naval history.

At the end more than 200,000 on both sides lay dead, more American blood than had been shed at Gettysburg and many times as many Japanese as killed at Iwo Jima.

On back of picture was written: "On Okinawa — happy because I am still alive."

President Roosevelt's sudden death from a brain hemorrhage was April 12, 1945. I was working at Rose and Buckners. All the stores in town closed and we went to church for a memorial to him. We had listened to many of his fireside chats on the radio during the war. Harry S. Truman became president.

The Germans surrendered in Berlin May 8, 1945. Thus, V-E day. Things were looking better, but Ray said there was still a lot to do in the South Pacific.

I graduated from high school in May 1945. We had many great teachers, principal and superintendent that all of us respected. We had a top-notch band, football, basketball and volleyball games, assemblies and proms. Life was simple and good. Because of the paper shortage we had no senior books.

When in high school some of the things I thought about doing was to work at the telephone company, join the Cadet Nurse Corps, go to college, go to work in Washington, D.C. with Mary (Washington, D.C. was needing and calling for office workers), or work in Kansas City with Mary. None of these things worked out. And, anyway, Ray wanted me to be in Marshall when he came home, and I wanted to be.

Jo Ann and James Albert Treece.

Twins were born to Francis and Fay May 25, 1945. They were named James Albert and Jo Ann. Yet another handsome nephew and another beautiful girl. Wow! Two at a time. My mother helped take care of them a lot when they were babies. That makes me aunt seven times; four boys and three girls. This is great.

Raymond's brother Nelson, who was in the Navy, docked at Okinawa June 1945 and at his own risk walked to find him. They slept in a foxhole together. Ray was back on Guam July 17th and they got to see each other again. Ray was training for the invasion of Japan.

Japan rejected the surrender terms offered in the Potsdam Declaration July 28th so the choice fell on President Truman to invade Japan, or end the war quickly with the atomic bomb. There had been a conservative estimate of a million casualties to invade, so the bomb was the choice. An atomic bomb was

On Nelson's ship.
Nelson and Ray.

76

dropped on Hiroshima August 6th and on Nagasaki August 9th. Harry S. Truman came along at the right time to end the war and see to the peace.

August 14, 1945
The Emperor announced the Japanese surrender.

August 15, 1945
Ray was on his way to Japan. In three days they were close but sailed back and forth just off Japan to be sure everything was peaceful. They anchored in the bay for two days, then landed August 31st. They were representing the Old Fourth Regiment. Needless to say, he was disappointed to be going to Japan instead of getting to come home.

August 16, 1945
Raymond's sister Dorothy and Howard Turner were married and moved to Coronado, California where Howard was stationed with the Navy.

Here I sit on my G.I. bed,
*   with my G.I. hat upon my head*
My G.I. pants, my G.I. shoes,
*   all is free, nothing to lose,*
G.I. razor, G.I. comb,
*   G.I. wish that I were home.*

They've issued me everything I need,
*   paper to write on, books to read,*
My belt, my socks, my G.I. tie,
*   all are free, nothing to buy,*
They issue me food that makes me grow,
*   G.I. wish I were on furlough.*

I eat my food from a. G.I. plate,
*   and buy my needs at a G.I. rate,*

Dorothy and Howard.
August 16, 1945.

It's G.I. this and G.I. that,
G.I. haircut, G.I. hat.
Everything is G.I. issue—
Oh, darling, G.I. miss you.

— *Howard C. Turner, 1944*

Raymond finally did get to come home, arriving December 13, 1945 at the Marshall, Missouri Depot.

During WWII more than 16 million served in the military. More than 400,000 Americans died while in service, 671,000 U.S. Troops were wounded. Millions of housewives went to work in war production, producing supplies and weapons for the war. They worked on assembly lines, drove heavy equipment and kept the economy running as manpower was either drafted or joined the military. In 1939 only 5,865 aircraft were built in the U.S. Five years later production reached an all-time peak of 96,318. The few tires that were available went first to defense workers, then to farmers.

A few from the list of arrivals November 21, 1945. Approximately 20,000 servicemen were scheduled to arrive at three East Coast ports aboard 16 personnel troop-carrying ships. West Coast arrivals expected include approximately 30,000 Army, Navy and Marine Corps aboard at least 39 ships.

navy. (Destroyer Carrol)—51 navy. (Destroyer Presley)—39 navy and 55 marines. (Attack transport Dupage)—145 navy.

At San Francisco—Approximately 15,000 army, navy and marine personnel on following: (Allendale)—2,033, mostly navy. (Calvert)—1,648, mostly navy, including ship's company for separation. (Bladen)—1,064 navy. (Fort Clatsop)—20 navy. (General E. T. Collins)—3,232, mostly army. (General John Pope)—5,387, mostly army. (LST 522)—15 army. (Maya)—30 army. (Mountrail)—608 navy. (Albert A. Robinson)—309, mostly navy.

Arrived yesterday:

At New York—Miscellaneous troops on following: (General Callan from Karachi, India)—3,162. (Pomona Victory from Antwerp, originally due Tuesday)—1,938. (Hawaiian Shipper from Calcutta, originally due Monday)—1,838. (Jesse Cottrell from South Pacific)—22. (Colby Victory from Le Havre, originally due yesterday)—1,938. (Vincent Harrington)—31.

At Boston—(Charles Goodyear from Marseilles)—499 troops including 437th military police escort guard company and 2nd evacuation hospital. (H. Richardson from Barry, Wales, originally due Monday)—27 miscellaneous troops.

At Newport News—Miscellaneous troops on following: (Nathan Hale)—19. (Hubert Bancraft)—16. (Anne Bradstreet from Naples)—114. (Cyrus Curtis from Naples)—22. (Benjamin Hill from Naples)—7? (Mirabeau Lamar from Naples)—(Pierre L'Enfant from Naples) (Isaac Hopkins from Leghorn)

At San Diego—Miscellan~ on following, al~

Marshall Depot.

Some G.I. Slang:

Gismo — Something for which you had forgotten the proper name: a thing-a-ma-jig or whatchamacallit.

Gung Ho — Battle cry of Colonel Carlson's Raiders-the 2nd Marine Raider Bn. Meaning "Work Together." Being too gung ho meant too much of a good thing.

Gyrene — A U.S. Marine, probably a blend of G.I. and Marine.

Hubba-Hubba — What the G.I.s said at the sight of a pretty woman.

Yard bird — A soldier restricted to the company as punishment.

Jar head — Marine wearing dress blues with stand-up collar.

Mae West — A life jacket.

Snafu — Situation normal (all fouled up).

Mickey Mouse — Petty rules and red tape.

Semper Fideles — Meaning "Always Faithful."

Helen and Ray.
December 1945.

79

IV

Previous Generations

MY GREAT-GREAT Grandfather Treece ran away from England as a boy and came to America, changing his name from Tree to Treece, I was told. My great-grandfather, William Treece, was born in Virginia and was brought to Missouri by his parents before he was two years old. They came by covered wagon and ox team. William Treece was a slave-owner, and was a Union soldier in the Civil War. After the slaves were freed, he took care of them for a long time, although they never earned their keep. One time before the slaves were freed he traded a Negro boy for forty acres of land. William Treece's mother lived to be 101 years old, and his wife's mother lived to be 99. The last time William Treece shaved was when he was married. When he died, his beard reached his waist.

My great-grandparents, Darius and Mary Harper Gregg, came to Jackson County and lived in a house close to Swope Park in Kansas City. When Grandpa was a small baby in a wooden cradle, the Indians came and burned their house, along with other houses. They were going to throw my grandfather on the fire. My great-grandmother begged and pleaded on her knees to save her baby, and they let her take him, but burned the cradle and all their possessions.

My father, Leroy Joseph Treece, and mother, Nellie Lee Gregg, met in May of 1905 in Independence, Missouri after he had gradu-

Back row: Lily Jones (second cousin of Dad's), Great Uncle John Treece. Front row: Great-grandmother Gillian Treece, Great-great Grandmother Louisa Divers Shackelford (Granny Shack), Hazel Jones (third cousin), Great-great Grandfather William Treece (we think Great Uncle John stood in for Lily's mother "Lou" who passed away when Lily was eight years old, to make the fifth generation). Lou was a daughter of Gillian and William. Both great-grandfathers, Wiliam Treece and Peter Akeman, fought in the Civil War.

ated from Hills Business College in Sedalia. Nellie Lee lived at 3314 Sheley Road in Independence. He was looking for a place to stay with room and board so he could look for a bookkeeping job. Mom said she was in a cherry tree when she first saw Dad. Not being able to find a job he wanted, he returned to his home in Sweet Springs and worked as a salesman for High Grade Made-to-Order Garments out of Cretcher, Missouri store, traveling over several states. He later went to business college in Kansas City. Nellie Lee and Leroy corresponded, writing many cards (Mom's hobby was collecting postcards) and love letters over the next five years.

I have a letter written by Dad 9-27-05 and 6-8-08 postmarked Shackelford, Missouri (he had been invoicing), 2-16-09 from Morgan Hotel at 315 W. 9th Street in Kansas City, and one 6-16-09 from Fresno, California.

Sedalia, Mo., April 29, 1905.

TO WHOM IT MAY CONCERN:

This is to certify that Leroy Treece has completed a thorough course in the Commercial Department in our school and secured a diploma.

We wish to recommend Mr. Treece as a thoroughly competent bookkeeper and clerk. He writes a neat business hand and is quick and accurate in figures, and is a first-class worker He has no bad habits whatever and we are sure anyone employing Mr. Treece will be pleased with his services.

Any favors shown him will be appreciated by the undersigned.

President.

(RECOMMENDATION WRITTEN FOR DAD FROM THE
COLLEGE PRESIDENT) Dad was applying for
a job in Kansas City, Mo.

Letter from Hills Business College.

Ohio Street, Sedalia, MO.

Mom used to talk about going ice skating, going to Electric Park at Brush Creek Blvd. and the Paseo in Kansas City, Missouri where they had popcorn, hot dogs, ice cream, shooting galleries, swimming pool, boat rentals, dance pavilion, daily free band concerts from a large music hall, and a large fountain in the lake.

LEROY JOSEPH TREECE

HIGH GRADE
MADE-TO-ORDER
GARMENTS

HANDLING LINE OF
ULLMAN & CO., CHICAGO
ORIGINATORS OF STYLE

CRETCHER, MO.

Dad's business card.

The Situation Reversed

We propose to you—

to let us make you a suit that will fit your form. Made-to-order-for-you. We don't ask you to make your form fit the clothes.

Light, comfortable, richly colored suitings in unlimited variety at low prices, on display with

ULLMAN & COMPANY : TAILORS : CHICAGO

MEASUREMENTS TAKEN BY

LEROY JOSEPH TREECE

CRETCHER, MO

Business postcard.

Also to Winnwood Beach Park (seven miles west of Liberty), a 35 acre lake with beach, swimming, canoeing, dance pavilion, board-walk, amusement park, and Monkey Island. There were concession stands, a three-story high wooden water slide, giant roller coaster and a three-story bath house over the water with 3000 lockers and a large diving platform, a fun house, zoo and canoes. The lake was fed by natural springs. An electric railroad carried passengers from Kansas City to Winnwood and other metro areas.

The following was written by my Aunt Leola, 99 years young June 21, 2004, as told to her by older members of her family, as she was only three years old when Leroy and Nellie Lee were married — my mom and dad.

Leroy came to Kansas City to attend Spalding Business College. He was searching for a place to live getting room and board. Walking down Blue Ridge Blvd., carrying a large suitcase, when Nellie Lee's brother Henry came along in a spring wagon, pulled by two brown mules. He told Leroy of his Uncle Bud Fogle looking for someone to help milk and do other chores.

Leroy completed his schooling in a years time. Henry and Nellie

Love letter.

Envelope.

Lee also helped Uncle Bud and Aunt Bertie part-time. During this time Leroy fell madly in love with Nellie Lee. She was working at Montgomery Wards at Belmont and St. John folding and sealing material in envelopes and addressing by hand. She also picked strawberries for Mr. Betts on Blue Ridge Blvd. She used a little six-box handled carrier and they paid three cents a box.

Electric Park, Kansas City, MO.

The Lagoon, Electric Park, Kansas City, MO.

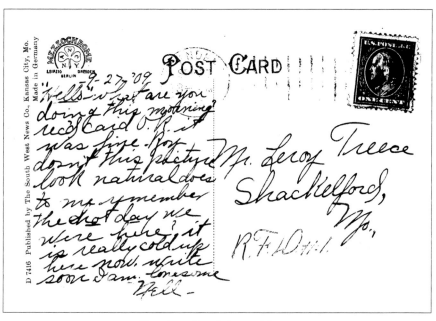

Card to Dad from Mom.

Leroy was not about to go home alone. Nellie Lee was madly in love with him too, but was hesitant about married life and leaving home. Leroy asked Papa for her hand. Papa said he could marry her if he would bring her home often. It was hard for Papa to even think of marriage for his firstborn, but Leroy was determined to win. All of a sudden they announced they were getting married right now. So they walked three miles from her home in Independence, Missouri to get a license and a minister. They were married February 16, 1910.

Interesting Facts
From Independence, Missouri newspaper 1910.

WEDDINGS
Gregg Treece

At the First Christian Church Manse in this City, Wednesday, February 16, at 3:30 p.m. occurred the marriage of Miss Nellie Gregg, of Englewood and Leroy J. Treece of Sweet Springs. The Rev. L.J. Marshall officiating. Miss Mary Gregg and Miss Fannie Fogle attended the bridal couple.

Mrs. Treece is the eldest daughter of Mr. & Mrs. George H. Gregg and has always lived in Jackson County and is highly esteemed among her friends.

Mr. Treece is a fine and manly young business man of Sweet Springs.

Mr. and Mrs. Treece left immediately after the ceremony for Sweet Springs where the groom has a comfortable home awaiting his bride.

Nellie's sister Mayme and cousin Fannie Fogle were their attendants. They walked back to Nellie Lee's home on Sheley Road where they all had supper, and still on that day walked to the streetcar at Englewood, Missouri (a suburb of Independence) about one and one-half miles, then to Union Station where they boarded the Missouri Pacific train for their future home near Sweet Springs, Missouri. Nellie Lee's brother Henry and her Uncle John Fogle saw

Nellie Lee Gregg.   *Leroy Joseph Treece.*

them off. From Sweet Springs they went by horse and buggy to their home."

Mom (Nellie Lee) used to tell about her feet being so cold and numb when they got to the farm that she fell over the step from the dining room to the living room, making a good impression on her new in-laws.

Aunt Leola said she could recall crying along with everyone

Home of the Smith's Stores Co., Sweet Springs, MO.

90

else as they were leaving, as Nellie Lee was like a second mother to her. She said Nellie Lee was the firstborn and always a favorite of the eight children, six living and two who had passed away in infancy from bronchitis.

Nellie Lee was very homesick at times and missed all her family. In those days people didn't travel very often, however they would call and receive calls on the big wall phone, with nine other neighbors on the line. Each of the family could talk a little bit.

Nellie Lee was very close to her brother Henry and her cousins in Raytown, Missouri, especially her cousin Ernest Collings. One winter in February, in bitter cold and deep snow, Henry and Ernest decided to surprise Nell and Roy. They boarded the train and on arrival in Sweet Springs walked the road to their home seven or eight miles, arriving close to dusk, almost frozen. They stayed a week, helping with the chores, making ice cream in a large bucket and turning it in the snow until it froze.

Henry finally got a Model T, and on his first trip Papa, (Nellie Lee's father) and her Uncle John headed for Sweet Springs. On the way it snowed hard and they thought they were lost and stopped for directions from a farm house along the way. Papa talked to a lady, and she repeatedly told him "this is Emma," meaning the town. He thought she was telling him her name and he said, "Lady, I didn't stop to ask your name, we are lost and trying to find Sweet Springs."

John Henry was born June 4, 1912. A cute bright-eyed baby. He was a good baby, seldom cried and had a nice smile. When John was a month old, Henry and Ernest Collings went by train to Sweet Springs then walked the seven to eight miles to the home and surprised them all and stayed one week.

John was three months old when Nellie Lee boarded the Missouri Pacific train and visited John's grandparents in Independence. They were met by his Grandfather Gregg, who was so anxious he had his horse Fanny hooked to the buggy and waiting for the train an hour before arrival time. Relatives drove to our home from all directions to visit with Nellie Lee and her new son. They got to stay two weeks. Leroy was lonesome and anxious to have them home again.

Nellie Lee was a very pretty lady. She took good care of her skin and used only Ponds face crème and talcum powder on her face.

John, Joe, Francis and Mary were born on the farm northeast of Sweet Springs. 1912, 1914, 1916, 1918.

Aunt Leola says, "One thing John and I got to do when I went down was jiggle our feet in the big water tank, sitting on the edge on a real hot day."

When Mary was a baby, Dad had scarlet fever. He had to crawl from the field to the house. The doctor said he wouldn't live, his fever was so high. He was in bed six months, but came out of it. Mom worked harvesting the crops while he was sick, while tending four small children. John carried Mary around and took care of her to help out. Francis was under five and he stayed at his Aunt Nell and Uncle Roy Crowder's most of the summer. My cousin Virginia said he was old enough to ride "Old Pet" and he would ride her fast and Louise (Virginia's sister) and her would get mad at him. Every day he would want to go to Cretcher for something.

Grandpa Gregg and Uncle Everett went down from Independence to help. They would get up at midnight to shock wheat and oats.

Dad got his first car after Rose was born. He

Mary and John on John's first day of school.

James Everett Gregg, WWI
(Uncle Everett).

Henry Harper Gregg, WWI
(Uncle Henry).

would drive his Model T Ford to Grandma and Grandpa Gregg's in Independence.

My mother's brothers Henry and Everett were drafted into the Army during WWI in 1918 and 1919. Uncle Everett was at Ft. Leavenworth before being sent overseas with the 89th Division to England, France, Belgium and Germany. He was in Germany one year and was gassed. When he came home the doctor thought he might have spinal meningitis. He had to be held in bed. It took him a long time to get well.

Uncle Henry was sent to Siberia with the American Expeditionary Forces, Company K 31st Infantry, and to Russia where he was a night guard. He took pneumonia while there and later had cancer of the lung. His funeral was the day WWII ended.

Aunt Leola said, "When John was six he would dig potatoes

and pack them to the house on his back. Joe and Francis kept chickens in water and gathered eggs. Francis had the task of keeping the reservoir on the big kitchen range full of water and wood for the stove in a neat pile by the stove." Aunt Leola would come in summer to help, and Aunt Georgia spent several summers there.

More memories by Aunt Leola:

When Leroy bought his Model T, the first trip was to see all of us, usually arriving early on Sunday and starting home about 4:00 p.m. The day was short for sure, but we all had fun. Several times Nellie Lee stayed with Mama and Leroy would take all the kids, Papa, Georgia and me, to the Swope Park zoo, and we raced around seeing the animals. It was certainly a treat for us too.

Sedalia State Fair was a big event in those summers. We all went twice that week, crammed into the car, some holding others. At times, John stood on the running board hanging on with one hand. Sis was up at four or five a.m. killing chickens, plucking feathers, frying in the big iron skillets, potato salad, deviled eggs, tomatoes and other goodies, big containers of water and lemonade, red and blue checked table cloth on grass, an enjoyable picnic, then to enjoy the fair. We all definitely had to stay together, which we did. Then, all tuckered out, and getting dusk, we again devoured the food and headed for home. I remember we sang songs on our way home. One in particular I recall, "You Are My Sunshine."

Rose, Mildred and Helen were born at Elm Ridge Farm in 1920, 1923 and 1927.

The airship at State Fair Grounds, Sedalia, MO.

AUNTIE

*A tribute to Aunt Leola — a poem written
by Elsie (Thomas) Treece*

For ninety-nine years
She has lived on this earth —
Since nineteen hundred and five,
The year of her birth.

June twenty-first of that year
She entered the Gregg palace.
Her father's name was George;
Her mother was Mary Alice.

There were siblings there:
Henry, Mayme, Georgia,
Everett and Nellie Lee;
And they named the little one
Leola Marie.

Then as God intended,
The siblings left home
For a job, or to establish
A home of their own.

Then Leola found herself at home
With Mama and Pop,
So she helped her father
In his big garden plot.

Then as she grew older,
She, too, left home.
She found a job in the city
And a small apartment of her own.
She was making her own way
And was living alone.

Then she bought a Model T —
How modern can you get?
And she drove to Sweet Springs to visit
Nell and her family,
She and Alberta Betts.

In a few years she, too, was married
And no longer living alone.
She had many happy years
With her beloved John.

They built a new home,
And she still lives there,

Keeping it up to perfection
For all to visit her there.

Then one day she saw John slip away,
And once more she was alone.
But she met life as a true soldier;
Nothing ever got her down.

She has seen many changes
In her ninety-nine years —
Some for the better,
Some bringing tears.

When she was young, she rode a horse;
Now they zip around in cars
Or fly in outer space
Up nearer the stars.

There were many nephews and nieces,
And God said, "I have a hunch
They'll need someone to love them,
So I'll leave Leola down there
To care for the bunch."

And that is just what she does;
She keeps up with us all.
She knows where each one lives,
And they all love her so much
For all that she gives.

So Happy 99th Birthday to AUNTIE
On this very special day.
We all say "THANK YOU" so very much
For being there for us
And letting us feel your loving touch.

We love you,
Your nieces and nephews
Greats
Great-greats
Great-great-greats
Great-great-great-greats
and if there are
great-great-great-great-greats,
them, too!
Elsie